# The

# Corn

# Wolf

# The
# Corn
# Wolf

**MICHAEL TAUSSIG**

THE UNIVERSITY OF CHICAGO PRESS
CHICAGO AND LONDON

MICHAEL TAUSSIG is the class of 1993 Professor of Anthropology at Columbia University. He is the author of many books, most recently *Beauty and the Beast* and *I Swear I Saw This*, both also published by the University of Chicago Press.

The University of Chicago Press, Chicago 60637
The University of Chicago Press, Ltd., London
© 2015 by The University of Chicago
All rights reserved. Published 2015.
Printed in the United States of America

24 23 22 21 20 19 18 17 16 15      1 2 3 4 5

ISBN-13: 978-0-226-31071-8 (cloth)
ISBN-13: 978-0-226-31085-5 (paper)
ISBN-13: 978-0-226-31099-2 (e-book)
DOI: 10.7208/chicago/9780226310992.001.0001

LIBRARY OF CONGRESS CATALOGING-IN-PUBLICATION DATA
Taussig, Michael T., author.
   The corn wolf / Michael Taussig.
     pages cm
   Includes index.
   ISBN 978-0-226-31071-8 (cloth : alkaline paper) — ISBN 978-0-226-31085-5 (paperback : alkaline paper) — ISBN 978-0-226-31099-2 (ebook) 1. Anthropology—Philosophy. 2. Narration (Rhetoric)—Philosophy. 3. Writing—Philosophy. I. Title.
   GN33.T38 2015
   301.01—dc23

                                                             2015015804

For Jimmie Durham

*For the songs and funny things he makes*

# CONTENTS

# AUTHOR'S DRAWINGS

*All other unacknowledged photographs have been taken by the author.*

THE CORN WOLF

# The Corn Wolf

*Writing Apotropaic Texts*

Truth can be suppressed in many ways and must be expressed in many ways.

BERTHOLD BRECHT, "THE ESSAYS OF GEORG LUKÁCS"

## Act One

An anthropology graduate student finishes two years of fieldwork and returns home with a computer full of notes and a trunk full of note-books. The job now is to convert all that into a three hundred-page piece of writing. No one has told her or him (1) how to do fieldwork or (2) that writing is nearly always the hardest part of the deal. Could these omissions be linked?

I mean—what a state of affairs! Here we have what are arguably the two most important aspects of anthropology and social science, and they are both rich, ripe, secret-society-type shenanigans. Why so? Could it be that both are based on impossible-to-define talents, intuitions, tricks, and fears?

All the more reason to talk about them, you say.

This essay was a talk delivered in March 2008 in a discussion on "Meaning and Method in History" along with a contribution from Hayden White at the Humanities Center of Columbia University. It was then published in the journal *Critical Inquiry* (Fall 2010).

Yes, but what sort of talk?

For is there not something else going on here, something connecting fieldwork to writingwork, something they have in common? For instance, fieldwork involves participant observation with people and events, being inside and outside, while writingwork involves magical projections from and through words into people and events. Can we say, therefore, that writingwork is a type of fieldwork and vice versa?

## Act Two

In a commentary on Wittgenstein's thoughts critical of Frazer's *Golden Bough*, Rush Rhees cites him: "And when I read Frazer I keep wanting to say: 'All these processes, these changes of meaning we have them here still in our word-language.'"[1]

Wittgenstein continues: "If what is hidden in the last sheaf is called the Corn Wolf, but also the last sheaf itself and also the man who binds it, we recognize in this a movement of language with which we are perfectly familiar."

What is Wittgenstein getting at? It is not altogether clear. He refers us to a movement or slithering and shaking that occurs in figures of speech, tricks you might say, which can occur with terms of reference that slip over into allied terms of reference such that cause becomes effect and insides outsides. Something like that.

The Corn Wolf is:

1. That which is hidden in the last sheaf of corn harvested
2. The last sheaf itself
3. The man who binds the last sheaf

---

1. Ludwig Wittgenstein, *Remarks on Frazer's Golden Bough* edited by Rush Rhees (Atlantic Highlands, NJ: Humanities Press, 1979), 10e. Rush Rhees, "Wittgenstein on Language and Ritual," 69–107, in *Wittgenstein and His Times*, edited by Brian McGuines (Chicago: University of Chicago Press), 1982.

When Wittgenstein says we are perfectly familiar with Corn Wolfing in the moves our language makes, is he de-magicalizing Frazer (i.e., offering a secular translation) or, to the contrary, is he raising awareness about the magic inescapable to language, meaning the familiar moves it makes?

And there is another movement, as well, although we don't necessarily pick this up from what I have said so far or from what Wittgenstein says in his commentary, and this is the notion of sacrificing a human being or animal standing in for the corn spirit. The person who binds the last sheaf is something more than a man or a woman with a sickle or scythe doing an honest day's labor. You can find intimations of this in accounts culled from late nineteenth-century and early twentieth-century Europe up to the time when Frazer published *The Golden Bough*, and according to Frazer you find it in many other times and places elsewhere, ancient Egypt, for example, think of Osiris, the corn god; ancient Greece, think of Dionysus. It is a momentous theme and Frazer spends two volumes on it. In an age of agribusiness and global warming, of environmental revenge following attempts to master nature, it is worth thinking about the disappearance of the vegetable god and its sacrifice. In the supermarket there is no last sheaf.

## Act Three

*A whole mythology is deposited in our language.*

[10E]

This quotation from Wittgenstein is what intrigued me for many years in Rush Rhees's commentary before I got sidetracked by the Corn Wolf. I have recalled it again and again: "A whole mythology is deposited in our language." It sticks in my memory. It has become part of my mythology. For this to me is the anthropological project: becoming aware of that presence in our lives, in our writing, and in our institutions, so as to neither expose nor erase but conspire with it, as does the wolf.

Always but always I find this Corn Wolf tugging at my elbow. I am writing a five- page piece on obscenity for a conference in Iowa, and I cannot resist my tongue-in-cheek title before I have written a word: "Obscenity in Iowa." It carries me away into the heartland on account of the contradictions this word "obscenity" contains. So I write a Hayden White–type annal, a diary of four days in my life watching out for the obscene, all the time aware as to the heave and shine of Wittgenstein's "mythology."

Or else I am writing about liposuction and cosmetic surgery as I hear ever wilder stories about these procedures among women in Colombia. I am enthralled by the desperation of this search for beauty and the elimination of nature by artifice. There is so much to tell, so much to consider, but what stands out most in the stories that come my way is the fairy-tale resonance of this endeavor ending in disaster, same as the stories of the Devil Contracts that I heard in the Colombian sugarcane fields almost forty years before, with both the Devil and the cosmetic surgeon providing stirring instances of the domination of nature, that's for sure.

Or else I am thinking of the desperate need for cocaine, the mythologies this rests upon and creates, cocaine that has now made Colombia into a drug colony instead of what it was for four hundred years, a gold colony, and if you don't know or can't feel the mythic power of gold and the fairy tales it has spawned circling around God and the Devil, then there is no hope for you.

And the wolf was there bristling hair and breathing fire whenever there was violence because if you write about violence, I found out quickly, if you are serious, it sticks to you no matter how hard you try to get the drop on it. Worse still, you so easily make it worse. How come? After all, common sense would tell you that writing is one thing, reality another. How could one bleed—as they say—into the other?

So, how much of a difference is there between Wittgenstein's mythology in our language and the mythic realities of these things?

They are exotic, you say. Not at all typical, you say.

But aren't they simple everyday examples of life itself, of the lust for life and cruelty, of the value and beauty that makes the world go round?

And nothing is as exotic in this regard as agribusiness writing itself.

Yet what chance is there for my anthropological project given the prevailing agribusiness approach to language and writing that wipes out the Corn Wolf?

Or so it seems.


## Act Four

Agribusiness writing is what we find throughout the university and everyone knows it when they don't see it. "Even today," wrote Theodor Adorno in his essay on the essay, "to praise someone as an *écrivain* is enough to keep him out of academia." You can write about James Joyce, but not like Joyce. Of course, there is always "experimental writing" and "creative writing," and "this is just a work in progress," as if all writing is not a work in progress. "Expt writing" is to real writing as the sand lot is to daddy's office. Licensed transgression.

Agribusiness writing knows no wonder, which—when it comes to anthropology—is really a wonder. Agribusiness writing wants mastery, not the mastery of non-mastery. Compare with Wittgenstein on Frazer: "I must plunge again and again in the water of doubt" (1e). Or Bataille: "I resolved long ago not to seek knowledge as others do, but to seek its contrary which is unknowing."

Agribusiness writing is a mode of production (see Marx) that conceals the means of production, assuming writing as information to be set aside from writing that has poetry, humor, luck, sarcasm, leg pulling, the art of the storyteller, and subject becoming object. Agribusiness writing assumes writing to be a means, not a source, of experience for reader and writer alike (see Raymond Williams's critique of Orwell, model of the English writing at its transparent best).

Agribusiness writing assumes the need for explanation when what is at issue is why is one required, and what is an explanation and how do you do one, and how weird is that?

This is the main reason for Wittgenstein's beef with Frazer's view of magic. Wittgenstein singles out the assumption that we have to come up with an explanation for magics like the Corn Wolf on which Frazer spends so much time. Wittgenstein goes on to say (1) we have this exoticism, too, this magic, right here in our language, only we don't see it, (2) Describe, don't explain. But then that's no easy task; witness the following: "We have only to put together in the right way only what we *know*, without adding anything, and the satisfaction we are trying to get from the explanation comes of itself" (7e). And (3) be open and be true to the emotional wallop we get when we read about stuff like the Corn Wolf.

Recall old wolf Nietzsche in *The Gay Science* choked up because in explaining, he claims, we generally reduce the unknown to the known because of our fear of the unknown. Even worse is that this procedure conceals how strange is the known.

Agribusiness performs this in spades. It cannot estrange the known, that with which it works, its itselfness.

He really lets his guard down, our old wolf, our would-be wolf, when he goes further in imploring us to love the strange, be patient with it, let it get into you, so to speak, and then you will learn what love is—and that will be how the strange rewards you. How many of us, you ask, have been affected like that by our fieldwork and our writingwork?

## Act Five

Agribusiness writing wants to drain the wetlands. Swamps, they used to be called, dank places where bugs multiply. As if by magic the disorder of the world will be straightened out. Rarely if ever with such writing do we get the sense of chaos moving not to order but to another form of chaos as with Nietzsche's dancing stars with chaos in their hearts.

This law-and-order approach reminds me of mainstream anthropological approaches to magical healing ritual in non-Western cultures, seen as restoring order to the body and to the body politic.

But isn't agribusiness writing resolutely rooted in science as anything but ritual?

So here's the point: Could agribusiness writing itself be magical, disguised as anything but?

Pulling the wool over one's eyes is a simpler way of putting it, using magic to seem as if having none, is what I am getting at. Here I think of so-called shamans using sleight of hand to deal with malign spirits and sorcery. What we have generally done in anthropology is really pretty amazing in this regard, piggybacking on their magic and on their conjuring—their tricks—so as come up with explanations that seem nonmagical and free of trickery.

## Act Six

Hardly a sentimental traditionalist or antiquarian—and, in fact, outrageously modern—Wittgenstein provides my anthropological self with a sense of Nervous System writing that agribusiness renders moot, cutting down the field in which there is now no last sheaf never, all sheafs the same, just corn, we might say. Say, dollars. Might as well.

Or so it seems.

Nervous System writing, what is that? It is writing that finds itself implicated in the play of institutionalized power as a play of feints and bluffs and as-ifs taken as real in which you are expected to play by the rules only to find there are none and then, like a fish dangling on the hook, you are jerked into a spine-breaking recognition that yes! after all, there are rules. And so it goes. Not a system but a Nervous System, a nervously nervous Nervous System, impressed upon me negotiating military roadblocks in the Putumayo area of rural Colombia in the 1980s as the counter guerrilla war heated up and reality was, how shall we put this, "elastic" and multiple, "montaged," Brecht would say—a fact that had been strongly impressed upon me by the spasmodic flows of sorcery and its curing by shamans singing with the hallucinogens drunk in small groups, myself included. Think of a Cubist drawing with its intersecting planes and disorganization of cherished Renaissance perspective. Think of a person changing into a jaguar, at least from the waist up. Or yourself outside of yourself looking at yourself. "The silence fell heavy and blue in mountain villages," wrote William Burroughs, no doubt thinking back to his time in the Putumayo, with that "pulsing mineral silence as word dust falls from demagnetized patterns." As I listened harder to my friends in agribusiness slum towns far from that sort of war and those hallucinations and that sorcery, I sensed how multiply real were their views of the world, too.

And what about me and my practice of writing? Wasn't I meant to straighten this morass of multiplicites out? A year or so later in my hometown of Sydney, for me one of the world's centers of order and stability anchoring the order/disorder paradigm we cherish—we have order, the other doesn't—I saw the grafitti on a ferry stop in the harbor. *Nervous System*, it said, ominous in its enigmatic might. A sign from the gods? A system on the verge of a nervous breakdown? What sort of contradiction and Corn Wolfing play of words was this? At that time I was reading the British House of Commons' Blue Books of 1912 with their testimony concerning the atrocities in the rubber boom in the Putumayo, Colombia, like those a little earlier in Leopold's Congo—over there, back then, our order, their disorder. British Consul Roger Casement up the Putumayo River reporting to Foreign Secretary, Sir Edmund Grey. The violence was too much to read, my mind shuts off, has to be exaggerated, but now it's not violent enough, whoa! where am I going with this, with myself? Only stories after all, stories Casement got from other people telling stories, and worst of all none of the motives made sense, leaving just violence, a nervous system there on the frontier, so many hearts of darkness and the ultimate violence was giving the Nervous System its fix, it's craving for order, at which point it would spin around, laughing at your naïveté because the more order you found, the more you jacked up the disorder.

Could it be that the stories themselves were the ether in which violence operated, the real reality? What then would be an effective critical response? Check the archive to go beyond Casement's stories to prove . . . well, prove what? That reality does not come storied? That you can get the story behind the story and out-story it? And what sort of calculus of utilitarian logic could prove that rubber, like oil today, was the root cause? At once too easy and too crazy. Or could it be that violence became an end in itself aligned with demons and magic expelled by contemporary psychology but ever present in *The Genealogy of Morals* or Bataille's visions of excess, the sacred payoff that comes from breaking the taboo. In which case my question becomes, What sort of story can cut across and deflect those violence stories, this being every bit as much a question of art and of ritual as it is of social science? The writer looks the history in the face at the receiving end of a chain of storytellers and has for a brief moment this one chance, the one permanently before the last, to make this intervention in the state of emergency, before the writer's story is swallowed up by the response it causes.

That is what I call Nervous System writing.

Roland Barthes said codes cannot be destroyed, only "played off."

But in this world "only" is quite enough. More than enough.

Hidden inside the last sheaf, the Corn Wolf knows this well—imagine the scene there in the corner of the field as the reapers close in. Think Breughel. Think Thomas Hardy. And the Corn Wolf is also the sacrificed, that never-to-be-understood activity, sacrifice, like the Nervous System itself.

Nervous System writing aims at being one jump ahead of the rules of rulelessness but knows at the same time that this is a doomed pursuit. If it is true that there is a mythology deposited in our language, Nervous System writing aims not at exposing that mythology but at conniving with it.

## Act Seven

I have long felt that agribusiness writing is more magical than magic ever could be and that what is required is to counter the purported realism of agribusiness writing with apotropaic writing as countermagic, *apotropaic* from the ancient Greek meaning the use of magic to protect one from harmful magic. This is prefigured in the wolfing moves alluded to by Wittgenstein, moves that counter the other, as in a Chinese martial art that imitates so as to deflect.

Wolfing moves include the following:

1. Refusing to give the Nervous System its fix, its fix of order.
2. Demystification fine as long as it implies and involves reenchantment. Glossing Benjamin, Adorno talks of trying to have "everything metamorphose into a thing in order to break the catastrophic spell of things." (Note the word "spell.")
3. The recognition that while it is hazardous, idiosyncratic, and mystical to entertain a mimetic theory of language and writing, it is no less hazardous not to have such a theory. We live with both things going on simultaneously. This absurd state of affairs is where the Corn Wolf roams. Try to imagine what would happen if we didn't in daily practice conspire to actively forget what Saussure called the arbitrariness of the sign. Or try the opposite experiment. Try to imagine living in a world whose signs were "natural."
4. That we destroy only as creators, says Nietzsche. What he means is that in analyzing and interpreting we implicitly build culture itself. And nowhere will this be more pertinent than with anthropology—

the study of culture. But what is also meant is the blurring of fiction and nonfiction, beginning with the recognition and appraisal that this distinction is itself fictional and necessary. That too is a Nervous System, the endorsement of the real as really made up. The ultimate wolfing move.

## Act Eight

But are we capable of wolfing the wolf? For as the sun goes down, as if forever, are we today not the last sheaf? And who will bind us? Truly the mythology is one jump ahead. For as the world heats up, thanks to agribusiness, is it possible that subjects will become objects and a new, which is to say "old," constellation of body to soul will snap into place in which writing will be neither one nor the other but both, in the Corn Wolfing way I have described in the previous act, the one permanently before the last?

# Animism and the Philosophy of Everyday Life

I am cycling through the Tiergarten in Berlin behind Bretta and followed by Thomas. It is a cold and rainy day in November. Yellow leaves lie thick on the ground. The way we sit upright but relaxed, breathing easy we seem more like machines than people, a collection of levers and joints like the bike itself. Where does the bike bit stop and the human bit begin? We are unified, this machine and I, like the Incan Indians in the Andes of South America were supposed to think of the Spaniards mounted on their horses not as a man on a horse but as a man-horse. Only our hats of different colors and jaunty angles give us away as something more human than a machine, something superhuman, perhaps?

I see some elegant cassowaries and then a zebra with its incredible stripes to one side of the path. I think, Well, we too are a zoo, me and Bretta and Thomas and our bicycles. What might these wonderful beasts think of us and our bicycles as we ride past? Do they distinguish between animals and things? What is the bicycle to them as it spins along, the spokes of the wheels catching the fading light of the afternoon?

The wheels of the bike turn effortlessly, not like in New York where people hunch over the handlebars and with a grim look on their face push furiously at the pedals racing against time. The man-horse combination of bicycle and rider is different in Berlin to New York and if the zebra and the cassowaries were taken to New York I am sure they would see that difference too. So where does the bike bit end and the human bit begin? And what is this "racing against time"? Is time a thing too, standing over and against us? Or is it part of an activity, like the wind on one's face while freewheeling over the yellow leaves in the Tiergarten?

Those stripes of the zebra dazzle me. The stripes are things in themselves that have come alive. It is impossible to domesticate zebras and use them like horses, Thomas tells me as we ride along. Might that have something to do with those dazzling stripes? I wonder, and then I think of the stripes on Genet's convicts in the opening pages of *The Thief's Journal*. Those stripes are the sign of a brutal domestication turning people into things, but the zebra?

And was there ever an animal more surreal than this zebra standing stock-still as we ride past? The stripes do not stand still. Not at all.

But then aren't all animals surreal, from earthworms to the snail and the domestic dog? It's a question of how you look. Like the bicycles on the move, those stripes of the zebra hover between the thing world and the animate world. Is it this hovering, neither one thing nor the other, that makes for what we call *animism*, just at it makes for surrealism?

Not for nothing does Primo Levi ends his book *The Periodic Table* by examining carbon as the source of life. At Auschwitz he worked as a chemist slave laborer for I. G. Farben in the Buna plant designed to produce rubber, and later oil, from carbon, the great symbol of which is the benzene ring, working tool of "organic chemistry," the chemistry of life that in this case existed side by side with death and the conversion of people into things and of things, such as carbon into copies of, well, everything.

Without this organic chemistry there could be no modern world. Most of what we live by and think by comes from it in one grand mimesis of nature, playing with the benzene ring.

What makes this the chemistry of "life"? Isn't all chemistry "organic"? What sort of word play is involved when we talk of "biochemistry" and now of "biopower"? Surely all these constructions are vivid instances of *animism* meaning a quality of being that is uncertainly alive with a mind and even a soul of its own when, from another point of view it is merely inert matter? And just as surely can't we say that the core of the modern world is animistic? It is astonishing how we so easily encompass such confusion and contradiction in our everyday philosophy and get on with life as on this bicycle ride through the Tiergarten. Only now and again does the animism of it all confront us and make us laugh and wonder or feel frightened and wonder, as with those stripes and the easy movement of our bicycles through space and time as our legs move up and down and the spokes on the wheels catch the rays of the dying sun.

A little farther along the path where we cross the winter-brown waters of the canal where the body of Rosa Luxemburg was thrown by the Freikorps in 1919, we come across an open field surrounded by pines. The field is full of mounds of earth, little mountains about fifteen centimeters high. These are made by moles, blind creatures that burrow deep in the earth, like the revolution coming into being, said Marx. The mole is certainly an animal. But what of these mounds? Are they animate or inanimate? And what of the revolution? Is it still animated or animating? Has the "old mole" lost its way?

The revolution would be surreal, too. And that means animistic. Neither thing nor nothing it would be a movement that took into account all these wonderful confusions that Western culture has created and upon which it depends—confusions between animate and inanimate made all the more confusing because in the everyday philosophy of life we use these confusions as if they were not confusing at all. As long as I am on my bicycle cycling through the Tiergarten behind Bretta and followed by Thomas breathing easy with our hats of different colors and angles, more like machines than people, it really does not matter where the bike bit stops and the human bit begins. We are unified, this machine and I, not as a man on a horse but as a man-horse eyeing a zebra.

# The Stories Things Tell and Why They Tell Them

I never thought that a thing like a burned match, or a scrap of paper in the mud, or a fallen leaf, or a rusty worthless nail might have a soul. The Yorrike taught me otherwise.

B. TRAVEN, THE DEATH SHIP

### It Is as if the Arrow Is Thinking

For seven months with his wife and teenage stepdaughter, Juan Downey lived in the Amazon forest hosted by Yanomami Indians. A few years later, in 1979, he made a video about this called *The Laughing Alligator*. There are many stories in this movie, but to my mind the stories are secondary to the filmic quality of film, to rhythms of light and shade, flicker and sheen. The stories are secondary to the way the montage of images tells stories simultaneously. And, of course, there is always face—the human face—and the near-naked body, all filmed in mobile and loving close-up wherein sound is enormously important, all the more so when absent as with the episode toward the end of the video where a young man binds a blue feather to the tail end of an arrow braced tight against the smooth skin of his shirtless chest, thanks to the pressure applied by the inside of his upper left arm. The screen fills with the feather set into the shaft, twirled slowly in irregular stops and starts. *It is as if the arrow is thinking.*

*It is as if the arrow is thinking*, inseparable as it is from the human body as both tool and beauty. First the right hand moves back and forth along the naked thigh, back and forth, rolling fibers into the thread that will be used to bind the feather to the arrow. The thigh is an anvil, a device for rolling fibers into one braided thread. Then the body becomes a vice, holding the shaft of the arrow tight in the axilla. Body and arrow are unified. Epitome of ease, the man sits as if on a low stool, his body the workshop of the world.

It is miraculous this feather turning on its own, it seems, reflecting many shades of blue turning black back to blue in the tautness of its being as the man keeps slowly twirling the arrow while binding the feather ever more securely to ensure smooth flight. You sense the arrow flying, taking you along with it. Everything seems so easy, unhurried, deft, like God signing off on the creation of the world.

That is the action of this video as a whole, the slow action of a magic at once technical and aesthetic, demonstrating Walter Benjamin's riff on Paul Valery's idea of the skilled artisan possessing a certain accord of soul, hand, and eye—that same accord that provides the basis for the storyteller as the artisan of experience.[1]

The art of the storyteller that Benjamin saw as having its origin in the traveler and the artisan returning to his or her natal village, is the same art that the traveler Juan Downey makes about Indians for an audience in the metropole. And is not Downey an artisan too, an artisan with a clunky 1970s portable video camera and monitor that he took to the forest accompanied by his wife and stepdaughter? But in this case the power differentials—Who is telling this story?—are continuously brought to the surface by self-mockery and humor as when the alligator of myth with fire in its belly is made to laugh and belch out its secret to the benefit of the Indians who have tricked it into laughter, a human attribute, after all. Thus does violence—the violence of the alligator, the violence of fire—pass into the realm of a story that makes us laugh too, wondering at the closeness of the connections between laughter and violence, like the connections between the comfort and violence of fire itself.

Later on we will hear more about fire—fire and humor—on the Death Ship, a floating furnace kept alive by madly shoveling stokers, black with coal dust and the fires of hell.

Fire is certainly useful, nowhere more so than for cooking the bones of the dead to a fine ash to be mixed in beer and drunk by the survivors. What a way to go! Downey is now dead but he is on record in his movie saying he

---

1. Walter Benjamin, "The Storyteller," *Illuminations*, edited by Hannah Arendt (New York: Schocken, 1968), 107-8.

wants his ashes to be drunk like this too, to pass into the body of the Other as "funerary architecture."

So who is telling stories nowadays? And who is telling the story about stories? Is there in fact a Great Chain of Storytellers, despite Benjamin's claim that storytelling died away with the demise of craft thanks to industrial capitalism? Benjamin's claim here makes it seem as if the arrow has stopped thinking and has flown away somewhere. Where might that be? Could it be where people work, not at binding feathers but where things, not people, assume the task of the storyteller?

## The Death Ship

Take B. Traven's 1926 account of a sailor on the Death Ship, a decrepit tramp steamer plowing the seven seas toward a rendezvous with death. Let us emphasize how Benjamin emphasizes the importance sailors play in storytelling as well as the role of death authorizing the storyteller. You get this in one swoop with the title, *The Death Ship* (*Das Totenschiff*).

B. Traven. Mystery man. Publishers never knew him, allegedly, other than a PO box in Mexico City. There is a story circulating that he was a German anarchist and writer/publisher of a radical magazine called *The Brickburner* who escaped to Mexico after the Munich Soviet was routed in 1918. He identified with the plight of the Indians of lowland Chiapas on the Lacandon side and in a sturdy, laconic prose, edged with irony and humor, wrote stories about their lives during the Mexican Revolution, twenty years earlier. (It is said that his history had taught him that it was not convenient to write about the present if he wanted to stay in Mexico, so he cast the present in the past.) Sometimes it almost seems he is one of the Indians he is writing about. Other times he seems like the seasoned revolutionary suspicious of all leaders, the Wobbly sympathizer who hung out with Sandino in Veracruz during the oil workers' strike, or the one who advised burning all the municipal records as one of the first and most decisive revolutionary acts, premonition of Snowden and Big Data.

Traven saw the big picture in the detail, like the global market in the labor in the mahogany forests of the Lacandon where fifty years later another revolutionary movement began—with the new Zapatistas.

*The Death Ship*, however, has nothing to do with Mexico but concerns a droll US sailor at the end of WWI stranded in Europe because he has lost his passport and sailor's papers. The epitome of innocence with an endearing childlike cunning—like a Brecht character or a figure in the fairy tales Walter Benjamin wrote about in "The Storyteller"—this good man without papers, humble to a fault, can't help but bring out, to the point of humor, the mix of absurdity and inhumanity in the routines of the modern state, especially with regard to immigrants. Arrested by the police of Belgium, then Holland, and then France, unable to take a job as a sailor for lack of papers, he is shunted from prison to prison, country to country. It is a farce. Does he complain? No. What he does is scratch his head in wonder as if on the planet Mars. He has become a thing amid things.

Month after month the French prison has him count and move things from one side of the room to the other, then back again, count them again, then move them again so as to form little piles of 140 items each. What are these things? They are "very peculiar-looking nameless things stamped out of bright tinned sheet iron."[2] Nobody knows what they are. Some prisoners think they are parts of a dirigible to be used in the next war. Others say they are parts of a machine gun, while others say they are destined for submarines, tanks, or airplanes.

Keep counting.

*Nobody suggests they might be something useful to mankind,* comments our sailor.

What makes the police and magistrates especially sore is when our sailor tells them he is American and, by insinuation, that because Americans saved Europe in WWI, they should help, not imprison, him. After several terms in different country's prisons he realizes his error, tells the authorities he is German, and they love him, especially in Spain, the poorest of all the countries, he says, yet with the most generous people.

Fishing off the wharf in Barcelona our make-believe German is hypnotized by the offer of a job as a sailor on a rusty tramp steamer that does not ask for papers. The sea around the ship is stained with rust, paint peeling off the hull. This is the Yorikke, the Death Ship. At once womb and tomb it appears to have been painted white way back in the time of Abraham of Ur of the Chaldees but is now layered over with as many different colors as are known to exist. Her masts are like "branches reaching out from a fantastic tree in North Dakota in November." [3] (Traven is aways trying to sound like a Yank.) When he first sees her, our sailor drops his fishing line.

---

2. B. Traven, *The Death Ship*, trans. un-named (Brooklyn: Lawrence Hill, 1991 [1934]), 79.
3. Ibid., 106, 107.

He cannot believe his eyes and bursts out laughing. But then the ship starts to tremble, frightened of going out to sea. "I could not remember," says the sailor, "ever having seen anything in the world that looked so dreadful and hopeless, and so utterly lost, as did the Yorikke. I shivered." [4]

The flag is barely a flag, pale, flimsy, and shredded. The ship's name can barely be made out, nor that of its home port. As for the name Yorrike? What sort of name is that? Just like Exxon Valdez, I guess. Or take the name B. Traven, not Traven but B. Traven. Names are important in this tale. They are like passports but none of the sailors on the Yorikke have passports, nationalities, or even names.

It is our sailor's job to stoke the furnaces and work the winch on deck that hauls up the ash. For the life of him, he can't work the winch. It is antiquated, cumbersome, violent, and unpredictable—so long as you treat it as a thing without a soul, that is. If you lose control, it will smash you and itself, which essentially means crippling the ship. Pushing its lever one thirty-second of an inch too far made all the difference. A sailor shows him the trick to get it to work. "I will say Gracious Lady to her," says our sailor. "Maybe if I consider that winch a person, then she will do it and work with papa."

"Hook on!"

"Heave up," came the call.

"Hello Duchess, come, let's do it together. Come, come, come, up with the shirt."

So there is a lot of deceit going on here, you say, deceit and conceit or at least a conceit—a conceit that rolls over into a trick as with shaman's tricks that involve sleight of hand and art. After all, what is a trick? Take the wing of an airplane, or a sailorman feminizing a winch suffused in ardor, hell bent on seducing the machine, now a she-being, indeed a duchess. With a wink and a nod this artful performance suggests a love relationship, erotic, playful, and patronizing, like an adult cajoling a child, perhaps a sick child, with flattery and a good deal of make-believe on both sides. This is how folklorists and anthropologists have often recorded their subject's view of spirits, supernaturally endowed yet sort of stupid and manipulable in ritual or with ritualized speech.

Yet in this same theater we sense desperation. Get that machine to work! Goddammit!

In any event we need now to focus on the trick—the trick explained

---

4. Ibid., 112.

and demonstrated to the sailor—which is very technical, concerning that one thirty-second of an inch. What I would like to say—what I need to say—is that this requires a skill as highly tuned as the man binding the blue feather. The body is important, as with the man binding the feather, too. The ship plunges and heaves. The man braces his legs. He is stiff, but flexible, his legs are like pylons but his arms have to be relaxed, striving to move but one thirty-second of an inch and no more.

We need to focus, that is, on the concept of the trick and its relation to magic and to things that tell stories. Maybe it's a girl-and-boy thing, too.

We might think of a trick as something fraudulent. But then, as with a conjuror, fraud too requires an exact mimesis of nature. Think back to the airplane wing. Think back to the blue feather keeping straight the arrow in flight. So we need to be thinking of the trick as something scientific and real, involving a scrupulous understanding and manipulation of things, including the human body in relation to such things. But as trick the trick slides, it seduces, it cajoles ("Hey Duchess!"), it knows and enjoys the leap beyond the thingness of things.

Is this why the sailor goes to such lengths to inform us that the winch is the same as used by old man Noah and that it belongs to times before the Flood: "All the little goblins of those far-off times which were to be destroyed by the Flood had found refuge in the Yorikke, where they lived in all the corners and nooks. The worst of these little evil spirits had taken up quarters in this winch."[5]

The stoke-hold is dimly illuminated by two heavy iron lamps—the same as the Yorikke carried when she was sailing to Carthage from Tyre in "the old days." You can see lamps like these in the British Museum. But those on the Yorikke use wicks made from old rags in the engine room and are fueled by spent oil from the ship's engines which of course did not exist in "the old days."

"The old days" is actually a talismanic phrase and phase that ushers in prehistory and hence the enchanted world when things spoke to man. That is famously Schiller's understanding and it goes along with what is felt to be a certain lack or loss of poetry—of poetry and ritual—in workaday life. But, you ask, has that really disappeared? Does enchantment not resurface under certain conditions, maybe extreme conditions, as in our contemporary world of machines, corporate control, and heady consumerism?

---

5. Ibid., 173.

Here you might do well to think of a counter-strategy, like what I take from Benjamin, of demystification *and* reenchantment facilitated to my mind by humor as we find with our sailor.

You might also think of Australian Dreamtime when—at extraordinary times initiated by the human community—prehistory gushes forth in the present and distinctions between land, animals, and people are spectacularly different to what they appear to be in the present. This is the same "return of the repressed" I come across with much of South American shamanism at times of menstruation, pregnancy, sorcery, and sickness in which the natural turns out to be supernatural, also.

The sailor's story is an outstanding instance of this and hence of what Benjamin was getting at with his idea of a *profane illumination*, at once mystical yet down to earth. At one point where he suggests that the storyteller borrows his authority from death, Benjamin says death sinks the story into nature or, to be more exact, into natural history. Yet such is the movement inspired by death that the story lifts off from natural history into something supernatural. "The lower Leskov descends on the scale of created things," Benjamin writes, "the more obviously does his way of viewing things approach the mystical" (106).

Is this why this ship of death tells stories to her crew? Nobody on the ship speaks the same language but they all tell stories to each other. The best stories, however, are the ones the ship tells. "The crew may leave a ship," points out B. Traven, but "their stories never leave":

> A story penetrates the whole ship and every part of it, the iron, the steel, the wood, all the holds, the coal-bunkers, the engine-hall, the stoke-hold, even the bilge. Out of these parts, full of hundreds and thousands of stories, tales and yarns, the ship tells the stories over again, with all the details and minor twists. She tells the stories to her best comrades—that is to the members of the crew. She tells the stories better and more exactly than they could ever be told in print.[6]

Let us pause a moment and carefully note the chronology of cause and effect here. First the sailors tell each other stories—stories about the ship or, more likely, stimulated by the ship—and then the ship comes alive like a person, retells them, and goes on to make up its own which are presumably compounds of the sailors' stories told over millennia.

---

6. Ibid., 131.

It appears that there is a web of interaction between stories and substances, as when we are told that "a story penetrates the whole ship and every part of it, the iron, the steel, the wood, all the holds, the coal-bunkers, the engine-hall, the stoke-hold, even the bilge."

What is even more surprising is that it is storytelling that animates the ship and keeps it going. The stories do this no less than the coal the stokers shovel into the furnace.

Yet it is class struggle and the worker-thing nexus that frames this animation, which is why the sailor asserts that you can have a ship functioning fine with a crew but no skipper, but never have a ship sail with a skipper and no crew. This is why the ship always takes the side of the crew, because the crew cares for the ship while the skipper's responsibility is to the businessmen who own it.

The crew lays claim to a different kind of ownership than the owners and the ship's officers. Theirs is an intimacy, we could say, an intimacy that comes about through their work. In *The Death Ship* it is not the sparkling sea and ravishing sunsets that feature in the sailor's tale, but labor below decks. The work-site is minutely described in a patient, detailed, down-to-earth way that without fuss or fanfare has nevertheless a visionary and mythical edge. Why is this? How can such opposed philosophies—materialist and spiritual—be not only reconciled but reinforce one another?

When introduced to his work space below decks where he will shovel coal into the furnace fifteen hours a day, the sailor looks down into it:

> The depth appeared to have no limit. At the bottom below I saw the underworld. It was a smoke-filled hell, brightened up by darting spears of reddish light which seemed to dash out of different holes and disappear as suddenly as they had come. . . . As if he had been born in this thick smoke, the naked shape of a human being stepped into the center of the hall. He was black from a thick color coal dust which covered all of his body, and the sweat ran down him in streams, leaving glittering traces in the soot of his body. He stared motionless in the direction from which the reddish lights came flaring out. Now he moved heavily about and seized a long iron poker. He stepped a pace forward, bent over, and suddenly it looked as if he were swallowed up by the sea of flames which enwrapped him.[7]

The most dangerous problem concerns the grates in the furnace on which

---

7. Ibid., 176–77.

heavy metal bars weighing between eighty and one hundred pounds have to be placed to hold the coal. The problem is that because they have never been replaced, the grates afford now only three-eighths of an inch support and the bars are always likely to slip out of place and cause the ship to lose way unless the bars are retrieved from the white-hot coals. Heavy seas aggravate this because the Yorrike demands extra steam and because the workspace bucks like a horse:

> The stoke-hold was ridiculously small. The space between the boilers and the back of the stoke-hold was considerably smaller than the length of the fire-channels beneath the boilers. Pulling out the poker from the furnace could not be done straight away, because the end of the poker hit the back of the stoke-hold long before the whole poker was out of the fire. Therefore the fireman had to go sideways and jerk the poker up and down to get it out. He had to do a real dance about the stoke-hold to handle the poker properly. [8]

Dance—as in trick?

In heavy weather the fireman was thrown about and could fall on his face on the red-hot poker or on his back on white-hot slags. Other times he would lose his clogs (they had no real shoes or boots) and step into a hill of embers.[9]

Yet—and yet!—the sailors take pride in their work and will never slack off. "They feel as proud of a job well done," the sailor notes, "as the Harvard guys feel when they have won a football game." Only no one cheers for the black gang. [10]

Of all the work, two jobs stand out; keeping a straight course and providing power, which I myself take to be the same as telling a story. "Some day when you know its all over," a fellow worker explains to the sailor, "you wish to have the true satisfaction of having done at least something while you were alive on this crazy earth."

> What I mean is, to stand by the wheel, say, in the dirtiest weather hell and devils can think of and then, in such weather, keep the course straight. That is something which nothing in the whole world can be

8. Ibid., 191.
9. Ibid., 191.
10. Ibid., 202.

compared with. No honorable trade, no matter how thick and honey it may be, is like that. Damn my soul. [11]

Is this the anarchist in Traven, finding a purity of being—a spiritualization of being—in the interaction of the human with technology in what I can only call an "honest" relationship with things, in flagrant disregard and thus confrontation with the demonic injustice of the workers' situation? Is this a replay of Hegel's famous allegory of Master and Slave whereby the slave achieves mastery over the master on account of his immersion in the practice (praxis) of work?

But in the sailor's story the stories things tell are not simply dependent upon, or evocative of, death, as Benjamin emphasizes in his essay on the storyteller, but on what we could call "the death of death":

> As soon as you understand that death is not an end, but only a condition, only a step between events, then there will be no more slaves on earth. And of course no masters either. [12]

This comes across vividly when stoking the furnace—the lowest, dirtiest, and hardest job on the ship. It is stoking that provides the energy that pushes the boat forward and makes it obedient to the man at the wheel. Maybe it's a shame that a good sailor has to shovel coal, continues the sailor's friend, but "it has to be done to keep the can going and somebody has to do it. It gets to be fun!" To throw six hundred shovels of coal and do it fine even in heavy weather "so that the fire stares at you in admiration, you feel so happy you just could go and kiss that mountain of coal." [13]

A classic instance of "false consciousness," you say. Too classic, by half. It is so "false" that something else is being signaled here and that has to do with taking work seriously and understanding how machines work outside of the ways by which bosses and foremen incite those below them to work harder. What is more, this type of work ethic assumes a society of equals.

We can sum this up by saying that loyalty to one's comrades in the work process is the same as loyalty to one's tools and the workings of the material world. It is thus a spiritual axiom as well as a material one. There

---

11. Ibid., 265.
12. Ibid.
13. Ibid., 267.

seems strong internal evidence throughout this tale and other of Traven's works to support such a claim which very much includes not just the value of physical labor and craft but detailed descriptions and insights into a worker's interaction with tools, machines, and basic elements of nature such as fire and the sea.

Moreover, if death weaves its shroud throughout, so does resurrection when, at the very end the narrator is left floating on the sea, having survived shipwreck and the death of his bosom companion, Stanislav, to tell us this tale like Ishmael in *Moby Dick*.

Traven himself is famous for his several deaths and resurrections, by which I mean his secrecy, his strenuous efforts to conceal his identity, his changes of name, and the persistent aura of mystery that clings to his persona. Indeed you have to wonder whether there even is an identity here, meaning one identity, apart from—and this is the point—the fictitious name of the storyteller; B. Traven, and his many books.

It is, I think, a wondrous thing when the craftsperson dissolves into his or her work in this manner, an integration, dissolution, and metamorphosis, which we see and understand in a precious and strange way when storytellers dissolve into their tale—as Benjamin says at the very end of his essay on the storyteller. Not just any storyteller, of course, but the "righteous man" dissolving into the story of his life which, it turns out, is a story in which non-human beings and inanimate substances come alive.

Well, this is one way of looking at the situation, and it coexists with what can easily come across as irony or at the least a loony sense of reality—operatic yet serious—as the gods rear up, especially Imperator Caesar Augustus to whom our sailor pays mock obeisance—"Don't you worry, you will always have gladiators." Happy? Asks the sailor. "I am the happiest man on earth to have the honor to fight and die for you, you god imperator."[14] Other times it is Imperator Capitalism. The idols have returned.

The fire stares back in admiration. The stoker prays to the grate-bars not to fall. The Yorikke teaches the sailor a big lesson for which he is grateful; "to see the soul in apparently lifeless objects":

> Before I shipped on the Yorrike I never thought that a thing like a burned match, or a scrap of paper in the mud, or a fallen leaf, or a rusty worthless nail might have a soul. The Yorrike taught me otherwise. Since

---

14. Ibid., 183.

then life for me has become a thousand times richer, even without a motor car or a radio. No more can I ever feel alone. I feel I am a tiny part of the universe.[15]

It is as if the extremity of work and being without passports or official papers generated by the nation-state creates an animistic world.

Yet it is not the extremity in itself. Rather, it is the skill and interactions between body and mind, body and machine, body and coal heaving that create or at least facilitate this animism. How and why this happens is, as they say, another story, an old, old story, including a fairy tale made of the merging of the ancient world of the great Flood with the sickness that is the modern world. When Benjamin cites Valery as to the coordination of hand, soul, and eye, required by craft, that is the same world discovered by the sailors on the Death Ship (which calls into question the distinction between so-called "unskilled labor" and skilled labor, no less than between unskilled labor and artisanry).

More than a thing-thing relationship, artisanry on the death ship includes at its very core the notion that work and the materials of work are saturated in a feeling for justice, both social justice as between equals and justice given in the characteristics of matter and technology, to what has been called "the parliament of things." It is the extremity of their situation, their dystopia, which leads to this discovery, just as shamans and great storytellers find their measure in a medley of death, suffering, and humor.

The "liberating magic which the fairy tale has at its disposal does not bring nature into play in a mythical way, but points to its complicity with liberated man," writes Benjamin in his essay on the storyteller.[16] But it would be hard to call our sailor "a liberated man." He is not liberated shoveling coal fifteen hours a day shoeless and starving. He is not liberated when his ship sinks leaving him, like Ishmael, adrift in the storming sea. It is his pal who is liberated, if that's the word, struggling in the water alongside him, liberated through death, eventually finding that one place to which you can go where they don't ask for your papers or passport but judge by other criteria. Our sailor, however, is left in the midst of the great nothingness that is the ocean. Once again he has become a thing amid things, having "let the

---

15. Ibid., 207.
16. Ibid., 102.

wick of his life be consumed completely by the gentle flame of his story." [17]

This flame is the brio—the animation—at work in every line of this tale. For what seems truly at stake is not only the exploitation of person and things but the conviction that the product of labor belongs to the worker, not the capitalist, "belongs" not so much as property but belongs as "engaged with" or "partner with." It is the worker who keeps the ship on a straight course with a good head of steam, regardless of official papers.

And this is why things are animated aboard the Death Ship.

## Wages of Fear

Things come alive in the 1953 film *The Wages of Fear*,[18] the title of which takes us once more into the world of wage labor under extremity as the title makes clear. Here it is not a death ship but a "death truck" that is the focus of attention as four men drive two trucks laden with dynamite over mountainous roads to extinguish a fire in an oil well in a archetypal Latin American country. As the tension keeps us on the edge of our seats, many things come alive, especially the tires of the trucks, tires that so frequently fill the screen that they deserve to be listed in the credits as *dramatis personae*.

I say tires but what I recall most vividly is a single tire, a generic tire, filling out the screen with its "tireness," the Platonic form of tires. Much has been made in cinema theory of the viewer's body entering into the cinema screen and just as much has been made of the movement in the reverse direction, of the image entering into the spectator's body. Well, these truck tires do that, in spades. Your body strains to assist those mighty tires that inch by inch make their way across inhospitable terrain. Your body starts to bend sideways and imitate a circle, urging on the tire which, believe it or not, you feel communicating with you along with the blood pounding in your ears in synch with the staccato rhythms of the powerful diesel motor of the truck. "There is no event or thing in either animate or inanimate nature that does not in some way partake of language," writes Benjamin. [19] You become the tire. You become the truck.

Of course the fear-ridden drivers covered with sweat are important.

---

17. Benjamin, "Storyteller," 108–9.

18. Dir. Henri-Georges Clouzet, 1953.

19. Walter Benjamin, "On Language as Such and the Language of Man," in *Reflections*, edited by Peter Demetz, translated by Edmind Jephcott (New York: Schocken, 1978), 314.

They are alive too. But have they not become rigid with fear? Their thoughts, like ours, are focused on their terrifying cargo which, of all things, has this tremendous capacity to come alive—more alive than alive—in one terrible explosion. Is it because of this that your imagination finds succor in the repeated close-up filling the screen, not only the close-ups of these gigantic tires but particularly and especially the dark treads in these tires, deep dark capacious tire treads that are like scalloped nests, homes away from home. A silly association of mine, no doubt. Scooped out shadowed scallops, they offer some comfort, a certain grip on life, hence more life, more alive, more movie, than anything else in the movie.

It is contagious, this transformation of mere things, such as tires, into living beings. Everything starts to tremble and metamorphose into animate being. Now the truck, for instance, shows its true colors. It is no longer a mere truck—if ever there was such a thing—but a prehistoric monster with its haunting siren and extra lights hanging off it like globular eyes that not only see but devour. Always, but always, we are surrounded by the throbbing of that diesel motor. When the truck has to maneuver around a wooden ramp jutting out over the edge of the mountain so as to be able to turn on a sharp curve going up a steep mountain grade, the wooden beams supporting the ramp become alive. They bend. They snap. And down below, very far below, we espy the lazy river that spells certain death. Those tires now come center stage. They spin. They skid. The truck shakes itself in one galvanic movement. A cable supporting the ramp to a stanchion higher up the mountain catches accidentally on a hook on the back of the truck. Agonizingly slowly as the truck inches up the ramp, this wire grows taut and the metal hook bends, you hear it scream, the truck advances slower and slower, the metal hook bends some more and, as in spring time, nature comes alive, only it is not daffodils blossoming but nature raw in tooth and claw that comes tearing at us out of the screen as the whole damn ramp disintegrates in front of our eyes to leap up and then explode in midair to fall down to that lazy river glinting below. Suddenly freed, the wire snakes up high in the air, a whiplash into the sky, one of Zeus's thunderbolts in reverse.

Along with the trucks carrying dynamite, the other great animated being is oil—and here we become ever so mindful that this entire movie can be seen as an allegory of the satanic promise of oil—as when one of the two trucks explodes, leaving a gaping hole in the oil pipeline running alongside the road from which, slowly and quietly, pours thick, black, sluggish oil. It is alive too, is it not, this *petroleo*? It contains the aliveness that shall drive the machines of the West. It is alive in the sinister way it oozes relentlessly like black treacle to fill up the crater in the road caused by the first truck exploding. (What do I mean here, calling it sinister? Only humans are sinister, right?) It is alive this lake of oil, a rising force that cannot be stopped. It rises higher and higher.

The oil is already three feet high, black and glistening. Like an invisible hand it claims the body of the man standing in it, walking backward, guiding the driver, engine roaring. The driver cannot stop because he fears losing momentum. Forces more alive than him compel him to gun the engine. The truck passes over the body of the man walking backward who has slipped and fallen into the oil. He surfaces, twisting like an old log, only the whites of his eyes showing in a body completely covered with sticky black oil. He has become a thing. The oil is alive. Not he. Only his eyes are alive. Not he. He has become natural history.

Now the truck is truly medieval, like the Death Ship, a creature emergent from ancient history passing, as Benjamin would have it, into natural history on its way elsewhere. The radiator of the truck is enormous, like the portcullis of a castle gate or the gaping mouth of a giant sea clam. Across the massive front bumper in huge letters is the word E-X-P-L-O-S-I-V-E-S, no longer a word but a sign. The entire assemblage is coming at us, a ghost ship advancing across a lake of oil. The thingest of things, trucks and oil, have becomes mythical beings. The driver cannot stop. The oil is rising too fast. Where are those tires now, those more alive than alive tires, covered with oil, deep in oil, finding their way across the hidden bottom of the crater? Here they are, emerging from the lake of oil, shaking themselves free as the body of the man crushed by those very same tires rolls sluggishly like an old log adrift on the oil.


## Story and Trick

Shamans in Siberia and the American contingent all the way down to Tierra del Fuego make mighty conjurors, we are told. They can throw voices, talk to spirits, travel the skies, and walk the depths of the ocean. They can extract strange objects from their bodies or from the bodies of the sick and just as easily make those objects disappear. In the twinkling of an eye. They can cure and they can kill through seeing, and difficult as it is for me to understand this, such visualization, so I read, is a bodily substance—like the down of newborn birds in Tierra del Fuego—that fills the body of the shaman. Such seeing is a substance and such visualization changes substance. Seeing is the feathers of newborn birds. What does "is" mean here?

Note that conjuring is not distinct from these supernatural acts but is the same thing. The trick turns out to be more than a deceit. More like a mimesis imitating natural forces so as to dance with them, like the snake dance in the stoke-hold of the Death Ship in a theatrical performance for the spirits as much as for survival. We saw that with the winch on the Death Ship and with the tires looming large and lustrous in *The Wages of Fear*.

With its love of rapid disappearances and appearances out of nowhere, with its turning insides into outsides and vice versa, shamanic conjuring helps us understand a little better how its "theater of being" presents being as the transformation of being into the beingness of transforming forms.

Animism. Anything but constant.

Stories and movies can do this too, as with a blue feather, a stoker on a death ship, and men ready to take on any risk for money as with the *Wages of Fear*. Things come alive in a continuous, if staggered, series of transformations as happens of course with work, and with the coordination of hand, soul, and eye involved in craft—including the craft of experience in making a story.

As I have tried to do today.

# Humming

*Taking my lead from Winnie-the-Pooh and F. Nietzsche I want to explore a site between singing and talking where the hum of the Great Bumble Bee meets the body of our faltering world . . .*

Bees hum. So does the traffic outside my window five stories down except for early morning when the garbage truck shrieks and groans, lifting and grinding, compressing and thumping. Interstitial sounds they be—bees and cars and even the shrieker—sounds that fill the void, sounds that don't really count, background, we might say, stuff for the likes of John Cage who taunted the line demarcating sound from music. A dog whimpers and twitches in its sleep. The wind hums through the trees and the river has a humming, cruising sound that never stops as it runs over the rapids when I go upstate to the land without traffic or the shrieker. And then there's the pretty well continuous ringing in my ears, the ur-hum, the movement of the warm blood through the inner ear, that blends with the outside world so as to form the one great hum of the great bumble bee.

I look at this train of ideas and images and am surprised at how they themselves hum along like automatic writing. They form a sequence back and forth from animal to human as well as from machines to humans. Most significant, I feel, is that the sequence as here written comes to rest where you hear your body perched on the membrane of the ear where exterior meets interior.

There are few bees around now, less pollination and less food, fewer flowers, and less green. The hum of the great bumble bee is not what it used to be as planet earth falters and the ringing in the ear gets louder. I hear screaming even when I sleep. Is it outside or inside or both? Could this be the bodily unconscious central to Nietzsche's notion of philosophy as the understanding, or rather misunderstanding, of the body?

Bees offer plenty to the allegorist. They appeal to me because their hum radiates through the vibrating heat of summer along with the meandering flight of butterflies, those other great pollinators, but while bees are considered industrious workers par excellence—the word "drone" comes to mind—butterflies are not. They are not industrious. They are flighty and they are unpredictable, a boss's nightmare. In their interaction with flowers, they are also held to be eminently sexual—as by that utopian schemer, Charles Fourier. So then, what of pollination, an activity as natural to the industrious drone as to the flighty flaneur, a butterfly if ever there was one? Does not pollination disturb our notions of work, implicating it with sex and vice versa to the benefit of what we sometimes call the "birds and the bees" and hence the generation of life?

In his chapter on the labor process in *Capital*, Marx writes approvingly of bees as skilled architects but faults them because they lack the capacity to create a plan in the imagination prior to building their honeycomb cells. They just act, whereas man is conscious of a purpose before setting to work and, says Marx, must subordinate his will to it."[1] And regarding bees, Marx had to reckon with that nimble-minded satire, Mandeville's *Fable of the Bees* of 1714 with its motto of private vices, public benefits.

But nowadays some of us wonder where all that human imagination, human purpose, and subordination of our will that Marx mentions have gotten us in terms of benefits, private no less than public? Nowadays both Marx and neoliberalism can seem deficient insofar as they neglect to question this alleged thoughtlessness of the bee, let alone that of the butterfly. Nowadays we are prone to be less certain about the distinction between man and animal as well as finding ourselves with increasing frequency wondering whether things have souls, and what it means to call a thing a thing? We ask more pointedly, What is an Animal? What is Man? What is Life? We might also want to ask how praxis actually operates in relating hand to mind and vice versa, and how to master the ubiquitous need for mastery we see all around and within each of us?

It is as if our humming is a conversation with the hummings of the world at large.

---

1. Karl Marx, *Capital*, Vol. 1: *A Critique of Political Economy*, trans. Ben Fowkes (New York: Penguin, 1977), 284.

Let us assume, for the sake of a larger argument, that pollination opens our eyes to the erotic quality of work as an interaction of materials no less than of the maker with the thing being worked on. And let us recall the vibrating heat of summer. You put your head close to the ground on a summer's day hearing a multitude of hummings and you see wavy lines of colored heat rising and dancing along with the hums through which bees patrol and butterflies circle while dragonflies hum as they copulate close to the surface of the river. Without shame. These vibrations of sight and sound, music and color, are turnings that to some people appear unpredictable, ephemeral, and may make you frighteningly vulnerable. Think of van Gogh's last paintings in which form surrenders to the vibrations of color as when he writes his brother Theo how the effect of daylight and of the sky "makes it possible to extract an infinity of subjects from the olive tree."[2] It was as if there was no such thing as the olive tree. It was more like a momentary artifact, a blaze of colors on their way to becoming blue flies and emerald rose beetles on their way to becoming leaves with that tinge of violet to be found on ripe figs.

All this humming, and this was the painter who at that same time cut off his ear and then his life as if the hum had become too much.

There must have been some humming action with Sergei Eisenstein too, as when he tells us that "Disney is astonishingly blind, with respect to landscape—to *the musicality of landscape* and simultaneously the *musicality of color and tone.*"[3]

But then what is it to hum? My *Webster's* dictionary is helpful here. It scans like a poem. A deep ecology poem.

As etymological reckoning the entry for humming gives us "middle Dutch," an exotic formulation, to be sure, the reference being the word *hommel* followed by the word *bumblebee*. Next comes an array of meanings relevant to today's usage, at least in American English. To hum can be to utter a *sound that sounds like speech* or to make the *natural noise of an insect in motion or a similar sound*. It can also mean singing with the lips closed without articulation, although speaking for myself my main interest is with that something that lies between words and sounds no less than be-

---

2. W. H. Auden, ed., *Van Gogh, A Self-Portrait: Letters Revealing His Life as a Painter, Selected by W. H. Auden* (Greenwich, CT: New York Graphic Society, 1961), 396.

3. The quotes are from another book of S. M. Eisenstein's, *Non-Indifferent Nature*, cited by the editor in the "Notes and Commentary" section of *Eisenstein on Disney* (London: Heinemann, 1989), 98.

tween singing and speaking. Humming is like alphabet soup, wetlands, where all manner of life forms thrive.

Of course there are hums of mine that are words such as

> You always will be welcome
> That cup of Bushell's tea

which was an advertising jingle on the radio when I was a kid in Sydney in the 1940s. But when today I sing this, which is not often, the emphasis is more on the cadence of sound than on the words which, to tell the truth, are meant to be picturesque and a little absurd. What we call a "conceit." But are not the days of the advertising jingle over as being a tad too silly for the serious business of consumer capitalism? And, to continue further with this historicizing, I doubt whether today young people hum and whether, given the ubiquity of the iPod, their membrane mediating inner and outer sound worlds, has the function it used to have?

What I here call humming was for me over twenty years an essential component of the hallucinogenic healing of misfortune by indigenous curers in the cloud-covered foothills of the Putumayo region of southwest Colombia, South America. On and off, this humming lasted all night and maybe the next and the one after as well.

There were few words. Instead was this stream of vibrating sound that set your body aquiver, a sound I sometimes thought of like the creaking of tree branches grating back and forth against one another in the night's wind. Yet it could change pace with alarming speed and now and again—and this is terribly important—would be pierced by unexpected loud clicks from the back of the throat as loud as a gunshot or else by a cascade of frothing sound from the beating of the curing fan of rustling leaves. Other times there was a whispering soft murmur like fairy dust falling from the stars.

This was a humming that got to you all right, deep into your bones. It is said that smell tends to obliterate the subject-object division, an epistemological quirk that fascinated Freud in his meditations on the causes of repression, as well as Horkheimer and Adorno in their chapter on anti-Semitisim in *Dialectic of Enlightenment*. Well, that shamanic humming I got to hear over twenty years in the Putumayo certainly played havoc with subject and object, assisted as it was by hallucinogens such that your body as whole, vision and thought included, would vibrate along with the great hum of the great bumble bee.

But then there were those crazy clicks piercing, as I said, piercing the flow, jolting you into another channel altogether.

Drinking *yage* several times with shamans in the Putumayo and alone in Lima in 1953, William Burroughs came up with an image that served him his entire writing career from *Naked Lunch* on. That was the unsteady hallucinogenized image of what he called *the composite city* which at one point he alludes to as "canned heat, great rusty iron racks rising 200 feet into the air from swamps and rubbish with perilous partitions built on multileveled platforms and hammocks swinging over the void."[4] Allen Ginsberg likened it to the view from Burroughs's window on East 7th street, Manhattan. The concluding note Burroughs added was that this city was a *"place where the unknown past and the emergent future meet in a vibrating soundless hum. Larval entities waiting for a live one."*[5]

Reading this I thought of Walter Benjamin's idea in his last writing, "Theses on the Philosophy of History," where he evokes the paradoxical qualities of the "state of emergency" as not the exception but the rule in which all seems deathly quiet and still, yet ready to explode at any moment. This is of a piece with Benjamin's advocating as historical reckoning the unexpected, flash-like, encounter of past with present to form a new constellation, "the dialectic at a standstill." Burroughs's formulation, of the unknown past and emergent future meeting in a vibrating soundless hum, seems appropriate here. "Larval entities waiting for a live one."

Put otherwise, is it too much of a stretch to regard Benjamin's "dialectic at a standstill" as a continuous hum? In which case his "dialectical image" is the visual equivalent of the curer's song, a hum punctuated by a sudden click as loud as a gunshot sending us off into a different channel, body vibrating along with the hum.

I have come to think that singing is close to divinity—a strange and perhaps banal thought, to be sure. By merely altering the sounds one makes with one's mouth and throat so as to diverge from speech, something miraculous happens. It is not the singing per se but the *divergence* that does this—speech in an Other key, we could say, where the angels fly.

Modes of singing that are like talking are especially fascinating in this regard because they estrange this estrangement. They throw the field wide open, as does humming in its quiet way.

---

4. William Burroughs and Allen Ginsberg, *The Yage Letters, Redux*, ed. Oliver Harris (San Francisco: City Lights, 2006), 51.

5. Ibid., 53.

With her *cantastoria* or *singing history*, Clare Dolan, the Go-Go Girl of the Bread and Puppet Theater of Vermont, finds a space midway between song and speech that, with some hesitation, we might call operatic. It is a capacious space offering many opportunities for contrast of song and talk as well as their mixing, and although there is little by way of rhyme or lyric, there is indeed lyricism, opening up the world.

Commenting on the sense of a "mystic potence" known as *orenda* in the world of the Iroquois, being neither a god nor a spirit but a diffuse power informing all things, the anthropologist, J. N. B. Hewitt, son of a European trader and Huron mother, wrote in 1902 that shamans have *orenda* in abundance, as do successful hunters and gamblers. To exert his or her *orenda* the shaman "must sing, must chant, in imitation of the bodies of his environment."[6] Indeed the very word *orenda* means to sing or to chant in the earlier speech of the Iroquoian people. Small wonder then that Hewitt repeatedly returns to sound, to music, singing, and the sounds of nature, as the privileged domain of *orenda* and magic.

Nietzsche would have been delighted. Didn't he say that music in Dionysian states of being had the capacity to intensify bodily states so that you discharge all your powers of representation, imitation, transfiguration, transmutation, every kind of mimicry and play acting, conjointly? In such a state you possess to the highest degree the instinct for understanding and divining, enjoying the art of communication, entering into every skin, into every emotion, continuously transforming yourself. [7]

Listen now to Hewitt and note how he uses the word "bodies" here where you might instead expect him to use the word "spirits."

> The speech and utterance of birds and beasts, the soughing of the wind, the voices of the night, the moaning of the tempest, the rumble and crash of the thunder, the startling roar of the tornado, the wild creaking and cracking of wind-rocked and frost-riven trees, lakes, and rivers, and the multiple other sounds and noises in nature, were conceived to be the chanting—the dirges and songs—of the various bodies thus giving forth voice and words of beastlike or birdlike speech in the use and exercise of their mystic potence.[8]

---

6. J. N. B. Hewitt, "Orenda and a Definition of Religion," *American Anthropologist*, n.s., vol. 4, no. 1 (January–March 1902): 33–46, p. 40

7. Friedrich Nietzsche, *Twilight of the Idols*, and *The Anti-Christ*, trans. R. J. Hollingdale (London: Penguin, [1889] 1968), 84.

8. Hewitt, "Orenda and a Definition of Religion," 35–36.

So might I be permitted in thinking that even my humming—and yours, too—is not without its quotient of *orenda*?

In 1938 in remote northwestern Australia in the Kimberleys, Andreas Lommel from Frankfurt was unexpectedly invited to meet with Allan Balbungu, shaman and poet. Disfigured by leprosy and despairing of his people dying and childless, he would sit on the ground and, holding leafy branches in front of his face, commune with the dead.

Lommel was told that when a shaman loses this ability, he lies on the ground and men in a circle sing around him for hours, humming

*mmmmm nnnn mmmmm nnnn*

For hours.

The shaman goes into trance. Spirits tear his soul to pieces and each carries a piece to the underworld. Deep in the earth, they put the shaman's soul back together. They show him the dances and sing songs to him.[9]

My Putumayo curer friend, the late Santiago Mutumbajoy says that the hum comes from the spirits of the hallucinogen, allowing the person hum-ming—*the person thus hummed*, we might say— to work with this power that lies beyond the visible. But like humming itself, there is no sure or solid ground here until the singer starts to hum.

All this suggests to me that humming is the connecting itself and not just the connection between insides and outsides, animal and human, machines and human, but the mediating medium—the *becoming*—that connection of any kind beckons to, if not requires, most especially in that special moment of space-time travel where imitation or mimesis becomes poesis, or change (i.e., where mimesis propagates itself into metamorphosis).

## Nietzsche and Winnie-the-Pooh

Humming implies rhythm, meaning first off the rhythm of the body in motion. When we walk and when we work at some repetitive task we may hum. Nietzsche was a great walker but we do not know if he hummed although, for sure, music was extremely important to him. Leslie Cham-berlain says after the death of God, what was left for him was music and

---

9. Andres Lommel and David Mowaljarlai, "Shamanism in Northwest Australia," *Oceania* 64, no. 4 (June 1994): 277–87.

color.[10] I wonder if humming should be included here too, along with Eisenstein's musicality of landscape that unfolds before and behind as you walk?

Speaking of repetitive activities such as walking conducive to humming, and vice versa, Walter Benjamin thought the art of the storyteller was facilitated when listeners were working at some mindless or repetitive task which made it easier for them to recall and repeat the story when their turn came around, storytelling being but one side of the operation, story listening being the other.

And with regard to stories, perhaps while you were falling asleep as a child some of you may remember that Winnie-the-Pooh is a great hummer and it is instructive to study his humming which, surely, has a lot to do with his love of honey, the stuff bees make. In fact his first adventure, or misadventure, is to raid a beehive in search of honey. He is a child's Ulysses, this Pooh of ours, always ready to outwit the forces of nature in the approved Enlightenment manner as he prepares an umbrella to act as a parachute so he can descend on unsuspecting bees.

A great hummer, he has a day job as well—as an inert teddy bear who makes a noise as he is dragged downstairs then upstairs by his loving companion, an androgynous child named Christopher Robin. Bump, bump, go the sounds as he is pulled first down and then, at the end of the tale, upstairs. Bump bump.

Yet in between downstairs and upstairs he comes alive as Winnie-the-Pooh. He is animated, we might say, and he speaks and he hums and he sings a lot. In the second chapter, which is when we get to really meet this transformed little bear, we read the first sentences:

> Edward Bear, known to his friends as Winnie-the-Pooh, or Pooh for short, was walking through the forest one day, humming proudly to himself. He had made up a little hum that very morning, as he was doing his Stoutness Exercises in front of the glass.: *Tra-la-la-la*, as he stretched up as high as he could go, and then *Tra-la-la-la, tra-la*—oh, help!—*la*, as he tried to reach his toes.

Here is what I would like to point out. First he hums as he walks. What's more, he is humming proudly, conscious of what he is doing, humming that is, and proud of the hum he has invented while performing exercises

---

10. Leslie Chamberlain, *Nietzsche in Turin: The End of the Future* (London: Quartet, 1996).

in front of the mirror. It is as if he is seeing himself from the outside and whole, yet the self he is presencing is something like an unconscious self, not necessarily in the Freudian sense of the unconscious but more like what I would call the bodily unconscious. Humming, we might say, is the happiness of the bodily unconscious or at the least its idling modality.

We might also note that this hum hovers between being nonsense syllables or sounds, on the one hand, and more conscious language, on the other, reminiscent of Futurist and dada sound poems, as when he exclaims *"Oh help!"* in the midst of his *"tra-la"* and *"la."* The exclamation "Oh! Help!" rises up. It is like an eruption in a stream of humming.

Actually the hum is longer than I have indicated.

Tra-la-la, tra-la-la
Tra-la-la, tra-la-la
Rum-tum-tiddle-um-tum
Tiddle-iddle, tiddle-iddle,
Tiddle-iddle, tiddle-iddle,
Rum-tum-tum-tiddle-um

What is more, as formatted, it occupies the bottom of a full page devoted to a drawing of Pooh looking very small and overwhelmed with his hands behind his back walking through the forest lost in thought looking up at the trees and the sky, somewhat like Heidegger, we might say, lost on one of those paths made by woodsmen and animals that go round and round.

As he hums Pooh wonders what it feels like to be somebody else. It is as if humming frees him up to think big thoughts and even become something else. Humming facilitates speculation and it facilitates metamorphosis, invigorating the mimetic faculty, the ability or the fantasy to be Other which, after all, is the necessary prerequisite for thinking.

At the beginning of this scene the narrator informs us that Winnie-the-Pooh is known as Pooh for short. This is an indication that language and naming are as much the subject of this book as are the adventures of Edward Bear.

Changing his name from Edward Bear to Winnie-the-Pooh is another sign of this. The name change represents the change from the adult world where he is known as a teddy bear, a neologism said to hail from big game hunter, nature enthusiast, and gung-ho imperialist, US President Teddy Roosvelt. But our teddy shrugs off this weird appellation no less than the name Edward so as to enter that other world of the child-fairy-tale alliance where he now becomes Winnie-the-Pooh and with this new name become animated, breathing the life of make-believe.

Games with language—or should I say games with names and language—are crucial to this book. And the fact that Pooh is the name of a person, or should I say of a teddy bear, yet is also the name of excretory matter, is another signal that names, games, and toys are plastic entities that classify and give meaning to the world, yet are prone to change the world as well, if we so desire, and hence they live in a permanent state of ambiguity, chance, and strategic misunderstanding as is the very foundation of the adult's imagination of the child's imagination, which is pretty much where Winnie-the-Pooh lives and why he is animate.

Such plasticity is not achieved lightly, however. Names and words are meant to designate one thing and one thing only. Look at what happens to people who turn left instead of right or are caught cheating at Scrabble. Yet to sabotage language can be fun and, what is more, the definiteness of language depends on its being transgressed—the role allotted children and teddy bears—and, dare I say it, the role allotted humming? We sense this transgression with Pooh's name which is scatology rendered sweet by the innocence of childhood. Occupying an inbetween land of considerable ambiguity, it seems doubtful that *pooh* would make it past the censors of today concerned with child abuse.

*Winnie-the-Pooh* is a book that adventures with language as much as with bumble bees, honey, Heffalumps, and the lost tail of Eeyore the donkey. That is why there is so much attention paid both to spelling and to pronunciation in this book which can be thought of as a comedy in language, at the same time providing a lesson in reading and writing, plying the boundary separating man from animal and kids from bears. There is a love of misspellings and of mistaken meanings of words, such as ambush taken to mean a kind of bush. *"Expedition, silly old Bear,"* explains Christopher Robbin. "It's got an 'x' in it" (112). In other words, young Christopher Robbin treats his beloved bear as he himself is probably treated by adults because he has his adventures with language too, as with his spelling and love of making signs to be stuck up in the forest such as his sign PLS RING IF AN RNSWER IS REQIRD (48). This is a rich theme. How many links in the mimetic chain of being are there, after all, linking adults to children and children to animals?

The singular importance of writing and reading as the subject matter of this tale is beautifully rendered when Piglet writes a message in a bottle which he casts onto the rising floodwaters, a message that is found days later by Pooh. ""Bother said Pooh as he opened it. "All that wet for nothing. What's that bit of paper doing?" He took it out and looked at it. "It's a Missage," he said to himself, "that's what it is. And that letter is a 'P.' and so is that, and 'P' means 'Pooh,' so it's a very important Missage to me, and I can't read it. I must find Christopher Robbin" (137).

That is what this book is too, a *missage* in a bottle thrown in the rising floodwaters of becoming— becomings between child and adult, child and animals, child and toys, most especially that toy we call language, both spoken and written, both heard and read. That is the *missage* of this book for children much loved by adults. It thus behooves us to think of humming as central to language, humming being neither conscious nor unconscious, neither singing nor saying, but rather the sound where the moving mind meets the moving body—as when Winnie-the-Pooh walks lost through the forest dreaming of honey and the hum of the great bumble bee.

## Hums and Cries

Many years ago Rodney Needham wrote on percussion in a memorable and memorably short essay in that arch Oxford style noting (a) it was terribly common at times of transition of an individual from one social status to another and that (b) he could offer no explanation of why that should be (he must have read Wittgenstein on Frazer, on the bracing effects of plunging into doubt, again and again).[11]

But when Pooh exclaims "*Oh help!*" in the midst of his "*tra-la*" and "*la,*" are we not made aware of a far more intricate yet just as common and just as momentous a phenomenon as percussion? For it seems that the combination of hums and cries is a "fact of life" like night and day, forming a curious dialectic with the "Oh help!" erupting out from a smooth surface and then collapsing back into it.

I say "fact of life like night and day" but there is body-seizing surprise and convulsion here as well despite such familiarity. Indeed, that is the point, this coexistence of routine and shock. There is a lot going on inside this dialectic, with cries acting like exclamation marks. Think of reading and writing skimming across the lines at a good clip—humming,

---

11. Rodney Needham, "Percussion and Transition," in *Man*, 1967, vol. 2, no. 4.

it be—then hitting the cliff face of an exclamation mark, grand chief of punctuation!

In a remarkable essay entitled "Punctuation Marks," Adorno tells us that an exclamation point "looks like an index finger raised in warning," and goes on to say that punctuation marks are like "friendly spirits whose bodiless presence nourishes the body of language" (shades of Hewitt on the chants/songs of Iriquois shamans!).

Is this why they occur so pointedly in the shaman's humming?

Let us review some of these dialectics here, dialectics of hums and cries, hums and shrieks.

The traffic beneath my window hums, except for the shrieks and groans of the garbage truck. The Putumayo shaman's hum quavers, dips, and ascends along with the trembling of his body, your body, and the body of the world, enlivened and reset by those "gunshots" in the shaman's humming like lightning and thunder erupting when you least expect it, spiraling you and the world into bottomless vortices.

A magical spell uttered in the earliest stage of gardening in one of the Trobriand Islands, east of New Guinea has "anchoring" as its predominant motif, as follows:

It shall be anchored, it shall be anchored!
My soil is anchored,
My *kamkokola*, my magical prism, shall be anchored,
My *kavatam*, my strong yam pole, shall be anchored.[12]

And so forth.

Noting that the first two lines of this spell are:

Anchoring, anchoring of my garden,
Taking deep root, taking deep root in my garden,

my sense is that the impulse of the spell as a whole is to root the plants in the soil which, so I wish to argue, through repetition, is the equivalent of humming, a suggestion fortified by the fact that at the end of the spell a forthcoming "portent" is announced, "*a convulsion which in native*

---

12. B. Malinowski, *Coral Gardens and Their Magic*, vol. 1 (Bloomington: Indiana University Press, 1965 [1935]): 129-30.

belief, is a by-product of magic." Usually this portent is lightning or thunder, sometimes a violent wind or a slight earthquake". Be it noted that in pronouncing the spell in a loud voice, the garden magician ensures that its magical force is made to "flow over the fields and penetrate the soil," and we learn, from many iterations, that magical power inheres in the voice — and I mean "in," like what Barthes implies by "the grain of the voice" and what I mean by "the mediating medium" that is humming.

It is fascinating to read that these great gardeners out on their coral reefs give vent to cries while gardening. In what manner they are "cries" is not told us by Malinowski. At one point he calls them "melodic cries," for instance, which butts against my notion that a cry is anything but "melodic." Indeed a "melodic cry" to me seems to bring us right back to that privileged space that is my touchstone, the space between speech and singing. A melodic cry would seem to be both a cry and a song, yet neither. We are given as an example the following "cry" uttered while planting the staple yams called *taytu*:

Kabwaku E-E-E-E-E-E!
Ula'i taytu wakoya
Wawawawawawawa . . .

Note the hum-like repetition of the *wa* and the exclamation mark at the end of the first line!

*Kabewaku* refers to a bird with an extremely melodious call which the islanders mimic with such perfection that Malinowski says he was at a loss as to whether he was "listening to art or nature."[13] I assume that the E-E-E-E-E-E! is that bird call.

The second line means "Thou taytu, sprout in the mountains of the *koya*," referring to a site famous for its yams on the far off mountain Koyatuba on Fergusson island—the "mountain of taboo" rearing high above the sea and shrouded in cloud where strange bird calls echo in chasms of what is then called the voice of the waterfalls falling into the sea, itself prone to changing colors as the sailors engaged in Kula trade approach its magical domain.[14]

Given this magical and multi-layered reference, it would seem that the

---

13. Ibid, 134.
14. Michael Taussig, *What Color Is the Sacred?* (Chicago: University of Chicago Press, 2009), 99.

"cry"—this "melodious cry"—is like a prayer in condensed and charged short-hand running all manner of poetic associations together in the one burst of sound as do the bird songs and the voice of those far away water-falls. Here there is action aplenty, speed and movement as mighty natural forces are, in the cry, placed side by side with the delicate tapestry of strange bird calls.

(In a note reeking with ambiguity Malinowski informs us that although not "really" magic, this cry is indispensable for plant growth and it is taboo to sing it before planting or at any time other than planting.)

Another "melodic cry" is described by Malinowski as a "chant," or rather an "antiphonic chant," sung after the work of planting is finished. The antiphony consists of a verse in what is probably a foreign language from another island, each line being answered by the cry *Yohohohoho* which he describes as like the neighing of a team of horses![15]

Here again the sense of a stream of meaning—the verse in the foreign tongue—being abruptly met by the "exclamation mark" of the "neighing of horses" is suggestive of my theme of "hums and cries."

With reference to "hums and cries" Father Martin Gusinde, writing at much the same time as Malinowski, has much to tell us with his minute description of the several month's long initiation that occurred among the Yamana people of Tierra del Fuego with whom he spent time in the early 1920s. He reports that in this initiation a deep sense of the holy in general and of spirits in particular depends on what I call "an aesthetic of interruption" in which each day a rhythm is set up among a group of people wherein a quiet humming and stillness of the body is paramount, yet changes quite radically in the late afternoon when there is an eruption of discordance, of voices and dancing, which, for some people, peaks with spirit possession. Let me quote what I once published on what Gusinde called "the extraordinary state of mind" created by this "aesthetic of interruption" in which humming is so essential:

> There must never be complete silence in the Big Hut, day or night. So, together with the "enduring silence" in terms of speech, there is this constant hum of a singer chanting, repeating a single word with a slight deviation in pitch. Instead of words spoken between people, there is one

---

15. Malinowsli, *Coral Gardens and Their Magic*, 135.

word sung again and again, interchanged with silence. In the small hours of the morning the humming passes from one person to the next, softly building in intensity and number of participants as the day stretches into afternoon. . . . People say "I can reflect best when I am singing softly."

By late afternoon each and every day there begins a dance that Gusinde would have us understand as catharsis, letting off steam after hours of sitting still in meditation. This is the time when people's "inner agitation" reaches its climax and seeks expression in voice and body. . . . Every so often a person is seized by a special excitement and moves trembling from one exit to the other shoving aside anyone in the way. The others say "That person has been seized by *kespix* [spirit, enthusiasm]."[16]

As I thumb through my papers and thoughts there seems no end to this pattern of "hums and cries," of vibrating plateaus seized and shattered by an eruption from within—hence the expression in English, "the calm before the storm." Perhaps this is banal and obvious and I am making too much of it and this cliché of the calm before the storm is an indication of that. But then clichés exist for good reason and to such an extent that we could say that the banal itself is the equivalent of humming and that the profundity within or behind it is what erupts. I recall Maya Deren's pointed description of the most effective way to induce spirit possession in Haitian *vodun* is the "break" performed by skilled drummers who suddenly alter and suspend rhythm. *Then* spirit descends—into one's body, which acts accordingly, strange and inspired, incorporating the dead now brought back to history's grand theater.[17]

Can I go so far as to suggest that Benjamin's "state of emergency that is not the exception but the rule" is all this, too? For here also we find that uncanny hum of the Devil himself, quiet and calm (on the surface), filing his nails and combing his locks while waiting to lunge like Elias Canetti's image of the secret as a tiger concealed with infinite patience waiting to leap on its prey which is then secreted into the enveloping mouth and dank mucosal folds of the dark intestines?[18] Hums and shrieks indeed.

---

16. Michael Taussig, *Defacement: Public Secrecy and the Labor of the Negative* (Redwood City, CA: Stanford University Press, 1999), 153–54.

17. Maya Deren. *Divine Horseman: The Living Gods of Haiti* (Kingston, NY: McPherson, 1983).

18. Elias Canetti, *Crowds and Power*, trans. Carol Stewart (New York: Farrar, Straus and Giroux, 1984), 90.

I see now how this torsion and rupture I call "hums and shrieks" began as a footnote or minor detail for me long ago, in 1972 to be exact, in the blazing sun in the sugar cane fields of aggressively expanding plantations in western Colombia. There I was told by my women friends cooking lunch for the workers in the cane fields that among the cane cutters was the occasional man contracted with the Devil who now and again would utter strange cries as he cut a swathe through the forest of cane, plunging ahead of the other workers, earning more money, thanks to the Devil, but rendering the entire field barren. Until today I never gave much thought to her emphasizing the cries which seemed to me an incidental detail.

As I write this I feel the sun and the unimaginable monotony, the itch of the cane leaves, and the sweat pouring, the men in long-sleeve shirts, long pants, hats, and scarves around their necks, like armor. It is extraordinarily hard work and they keep at it eight to ten hours, day after day. Even though there is continuous alteration in the speed and movement of their bodies and of the flashing machete, there is also a rhythm to their working and as I write I hear the hum of that work shimmering in the fierce sun; the steady cutting of leaves, then the stalks, and the barely perceptible thud as the stalks are thrown into a pile.

But the screams? What of the screams?

I do not know. But what I want to suggest is that the scream is part of an opera, signature of the contract with the prince of darkness uniting soil and sky in the unholy matrimony we nowadays call agribusiness. It is like lightning and might I also suggest—I am not above making my own cries, after all—that the cry is also signature of that moment in history when long-established "pre-capitalist" rhythms of labor and use of the body are appropriated by agribusiness converting the human body into a bio-machine creeping along the unnaturally flat expanse of the vast sugar cane fields. If you look at the flexed upper arm of someone who has been working several years as a cane cutter or loader you will be surprised to see that what should normally be a smooth ellipsoid mass of biceps is instead a square or rectangular block like a block of wood. It is astonishing to see this block of wood ascending and descending, emerging and disappearing, as the man flexes his arm or what you thought of as his arm.

If my suggestions appear melodramatic and in themselves "operatic," take the workers standing up to their chests in vats of stinking, fermenting, indigo liquid under the hot sky of British Bengal in the 1850s. For hours at a time they beat the blue-green liquid with paddles, thereby oxygenating it so the chemical reaction necessary to make indigo dye can take place. They work collectively, in unison, maybe fifteen men to a vat, standing close to one another and working not just with each other but with the swirling back and forth of the liquid. Girded by a necklace of blue foam a foot high, the vat is in violent commotion.

As they advance and retreat along with this incandescent wave, their bodies blue, the workers sing what my British eyewitness, name of Colesworthy Grant, says are obscene songs and they give voice to vehement cries. [19] Here the record halts. We can go no further. Why obscene? we ask. Why songs? And why the vehement cries?

As for obscene songs sung while working, I also recall Laura Bohannan describing women working collectively, weeding in Tiv land in Nigeria in the 1950s. Men were frightened to get too close to the women singing lusty songs for fear of sexual molestation. [20]

Women weeding collectively in the Trobriands "enjoy special privileges" says Malinowski. Men must not approach them and in the south of the island where he lived women can seize and mishandle any man in sight. If he is from their own community, they merely insult him verbally but if a stranger he might be "ill treated in a sexually degrading manner." What is more some of the gardening songs are "somewhat obscene," likening planting, for instance, to sexual intercourse and the soil to the wide open vulva. [21]

With respect to the West Indian work songs she collected in the Panama Canal Zone in the 1940s, Louise Cramer tells us that many "of them are too obscene for inclusion." In one instance she came across a carpenter dancing and singing while planning wood. [22]

African American laboring men in the US before and after slavery seem to have had many such songs. In the Gandy Dancer crews maintaining the railroads in the video I have seen, you hear the rhythmic cadence and then the grunt or "cry" as the collective force is applied. It is impossible to convey this in words alone because so much depends on voice and the music therein, but two things stand out for me; one is the sexualization ("slide

---

19. Colesworthy Grant, *Rural Life In Bengal* (Calcutta: Bibhash Gupta, 1984 [1864]), 129. The passage reads: "The operation of the beating continues for about two hours—the men amusing themselves and encouraging each other the while by sundry vehement cries and songs—generally not particularly distinguished for elegance or purity."

20. See Laura Bohannan (pseudonym Elenore Smith Bowen), *Return to Laughter* (New York: Random House, 1964 [1954]), 75–76.

21. Malinowski, Coral Gardens and Their Magic, 135–36; 140.

22. Louise Cramer, "Songs of West Indian Negroes in the Canal Zone," *California Folklore Quarterly* 5, no. 3 (July 1946): 245.

them in/ slide them out," "I can make your belly grow," "I don't know, but I been told/ Suzie has a jelly roll") and the other is singing to otherwise inert matter such as railroad spikes as if they are people.

"Gandy Dancer" seems to say it all. Gandy was the name of the factory that made the tools such as the crow bar, while Dancer refers to the laborers "dancing" their way into materiality through "hums and cries." The very name of the iron tool, *Gandy*, well conveys this coalescence of the animate with the inanimate, of inertness with lively life. Where would southern slavery and the black foundations of industrial capitalism have gotten without appropriations of tradition such as this appropriation of "hums and cries?

## A Magical Snare

It is often said by scholars that singing, especially collective singing, makes labor more efficient by facilitating coordination between workers, diminishing boredom and—given that most labor is carried out for a boss or rich person—helps keep the workers in line even when the songs sound rebellious. As a young boy aged about seven I marveled at the marching Australian troops near my home who would be singing as they marched:

I had a good job for twenty five bob
And I socked the manager in the gob
With a left,
A left,
A left, right, left

But what is "efficiency"?

Following the many German theories of work rhythm, such as that of Karl Bucher, around the time of WWI, Malinowski made a detailed argument to the effect that in much the same way as collective singing, magic organized communal labor in the Trobriand islands.[23] He had in mind the big picture of the agricultural timetable, it being magic in the form of group rituals staged at discrete intervals, so he claimed, that orchestrated the work in a sequence in accord with the demands of nature—rainfall, weed growth, etc.—and coordinated the several workers into the one group

---

23. See Michael Cowan, *Technology's Pulse: Essays on Rhythm in German Modernism* (London: IGRS, University of London, 2011).

instrument. This is one reason why his books contain many time charts. Yet as he is at pains to point out, the islanders are not short on knowledge of agriculture and are hardly in need of a magician to tell them what to do and when to do it. More persuasive is the claim for aesthetics and performance in work itself, such that we can see the magician as orchestrating a large-scale "happening" out there on the coral gardens and their magic. This fusion of work with beauty is not an easy idea for us moderns to understand or digest, nor is the possibility that the beauty of growing plants feeds into the aesthetic creations of song, dance, body painting, house and canoe construction, and it is this that makes them satisfying, beautiful, *and* efficient.

What is more, utilitarian explanations of such magic minimize or even ignore the possibility, or point of view, that song per se, either collective or solo, like incantation (by which I mean magical speech as with spells and prayers), can in itself be an engagement with the material life of things, uniting, so to speak, the human body with other bodies and the body of the world through the bodily unconscious.

Malinowski emphasizes the communal character of labor in the Trobriand gardens, yet seems oblivious to an outstanding element of such communality, and that is the participation of the plants themselves as sentient, human-like, beings. As one of the islanders tells him, "We plant taytu, already it lies (in the ground); later on, it hears magic above, already it sprouts" (141). Like most anthropologists he is caught in a conflict of philosophies or ontologies; on the one hand the modern European view of nature as an object, not a subject, in some sense dead and distant, and this other view which understands nature in human and spiritual terms as a subject, too.

## Okay, but What about the Obscenity?

What I would like to propose is that we understand obscenity as not only transgression of boundaries, defined in terms of the more obvious erotic zones, but as transgression of bodily propriety more generally understood—by which I mean the "sexualized" body of the world including, of course, the human body within that body.

I am thinking of Bataille's dense analysis of erotism as a specific manner of transgressing taboo, finding that strange, charged, space of being that is created by setting the taboo aside. When thinkers such as Malinowski beat us over the head with utilitarian explanations of magic in gardening or in the construction of a canoe, they are a long way from this point of view: that "magic," as I see it—as I am arguing here—is an entailment, a script, if you like, of just such a transgressed "space" and required by it.

As with the bees and the butterflies evoked at the beginning of this essay, it seems like working in nature is to partake sexually, so to speak, with the libidinal life of materials. In the indigo vat it is the density and intimacy of the interaction with the inner life of the object world that astounds me, whether it be the harmonies and self-transforming movements of animating materials confined by the vat, or whether it be their exploding into obscene song and color. All labor has something of this quality—this eerie intimacy with things and with motions inseparable from the thing we call mind, only we take it for granted and rarely notice it until hit with a broadside from the colonies and from sites of manual labor where the mix of horror and the fabulous makes us sit up and take note. Magic is sometimes said to be just this dazzling fusion of the human with the thing world too, although the work is likely to be more involved with theater and incantation. The *collective* nature of the work I have cited in the Bengal vat or Trobriand gardens makes this magical movement and fusion with the intimacy of the material world all the more noticeable, especially when the bodies move like one as in a chorus line in time to the music which brings the social and the natural worlds together.

In his relentless analysis of the famous dancing troupe, the Tiller Girls, Siegfried Kracauer, leaves no stone unturned in arguing that that their collective, unified, movements are analogs of industrial labor in which the body has itself become a slave-like extension of the machine. [24] Not much room here, you might say, for what I call the "eerie intimacy of things." But think again!

The magic is there in spades. It is literally spellbinding to witness the human bodies perform as do these scantily dressed Tiller Girls all in a line, legs high, in perfect unison, a spell that has as much to do with what I assume to be our never-ending appreciation of the immense mimetic capabilities of the human body. Here the female body performs the machine (and is not just *like* a machine). What is more, although Kracauer minimizes the erotic charge these dancers emit, it is as present there as

---

24. Siegfried Kracauer's *The Mass Ornament: Weimar Essays*, trans. Thomas Y. Levin (Cambridge, MA: Harvard University Press, 1995).

it is in "the obscene" presenced in Tiv land and with Trobriand women's collective weeding.

As I watch these harmonious legs all in unison, I cannot but refer once more to humming and think of Nietzsche, who loved moving his legs too, walking every day as part of his thinking. I see him pointing to the age-old magical power of rhythm, not only in prayer as a magical snare to make the gods pliable, but in mundane activities as well, such as rowing or bailing water from a boat. Still today, he thought, even "after millennia of work at fighting such superstition," this magical power of rhythm exerts itself.[25]

So I ask myself, is humming, then, a "magical snare" too, a rhythm of sounds without words making a prayer without any obvious church or priest? Can humming snare the violence of state, as well, where William Burroughs's "unknown past and the emergent future meet in a vibrating soundless hum?

MR. WEINGLASS: Will you please state your full name?
THE WITNESS: Allen Ginsberg.
MR. WEINGLASS: What is your Occupation?
THE WITNESS: Poet.
THE WITNESS: I was chanting a mantra called the "Mala Mantra," the great mantra of preservation of that aspect of the Indian religion called Vishnu the Preserver. Every time human evil rises so high that the planet itself is threatened, and all of its inhabitants and their children are threatened, Vishnu will preserve a return.
MR. WEINGLASS: And what occurred in Lincoln Park at approximately 10:30, if you can recall?
THE WITNESS: There were several thousand young people gathered, waiting, late at night. It was dark. There were some bonfires burning in trashcans. Everybody was standing around not knowing what to do. Suddenly there was a great deal of consternation and movement and shouting among the crowd in the park, and I turned, surprised, because it was early. The police were or had given 11:00 as the date or as the time—
MR. FORAN: Objection, your Honor.
MR. WEINGLASS: What did you do at the time you saw the police do this?

---

25. Friedrich Nietzsche, *The Gay Science*, trans. Josefine Nauckhoff and Adrian Del Caro (Cambridge: Cambridge University Press, 2001), 84: 83–86.

THE WITNESS: I started the chant, O-o-m-m-m-m-m-, O-o-m-m-m-m-m-m.

MR. FORAN: All right, we have had a demonstration.

THE COURT: All right.

MR. WEINGLASS : Did you finish your answer?

THE WITNESS: We walked out of the park. We continued chanting for at least twenty minutes, slowly gathering other people, chanting, Ed Sanders and I in the center, until there was a group of maybe fifteen or twenty making a very solid heavy vibrational change of aim that penetrated the immediate area around us, and attracted other people, and so we walked out slowly toward the street, toward Lincoln Park.

MR. WEINGLASS: I now show you what is marked D-153 for identification. Could you read that to the jury?

THE WITNESS: Magic Password Bulletin. Physic Jujitsu. In case of hysteria, the magic password is o-m, same as o-h-m-, which cuts through all emergency illusions. Pronounce o-m from the middle of the body, diaphragm or solar plexus. Ten people humming o-m can calm down one himself. One hundred people humming o-m can regulate the metabolism of a thousand. A thousand bodies vibrating o-m can immobilize an entire downtown Chicago street full of scared humans, uniformed or naked. Signed, Allen Ginsberg, Ed Sanders. O-m will be practiced on the beach at sunrise ceremonies with Allen and Ed.

MR. WEINGLASS: Could you explain to the Court and jury what you meant in that last statement of your message?

THE WITNESS: By "immobilize" I meant shut down the mental machinery which repeats over and over again the images of fear which are scaring people in uniform—that is to say, the police officers or the demonstrators, whom I refer to as naked meaning naked emotionally, and perhaps hopefully naked physically.

MR. WEINGLASS: And what did you intend to create by having that mechanism shut down?

THE WITNESS: A completely peaceful realization of the fact that we were all stuck in the same street, place, terrified of each other, and reacting in panic and hysteria rather than reacting with awareness of each other as human beings, as people with bodies that actually feel, can chant and pray and have a certain sense of' vibration to each other or tenderness to each other which is basically what everybody wants, rather than fear.

MR. WEINGLASS: Now directing your attention to the next day which is Sunday, August 25th, what, if anything, did you do in the park?

THE WITNESS: First I walked around to the center of the park, where suddenly a group of policemen appeared in the middle of the younger people. There was an appearance of a great mass of policemen going through the center of the park. I was afraid then, thinking they were going to make trouble—

MR. FORAN: Objection to his state of mind.

THE COURT: I sustain the objection.

MR. WEINGLASS: What did you do when you saw the policemen in the center of the crowd?

THE WITNESS: Adrenalin ran through my body. I sat down on a green hillside with a group of younger people that were walking with me about 3:30 in the afternoon, 4:00 o'clock. Sat, crossed my legs, and began chanting O-o-m—-O-o—m-m-m-m, O-o-m-m-m-m, O-o-m-m-m-m-m.

MR. FORAN: I gave him four that time.

THE WITNESS: I continued chanting for several hours.

THE COURT: Did you say you continued chanting seven hours?

THE WITNESS: Seven hours, yes. About six hours I chanted "Om" and for the seventh hour concluded with the chant Hare krishna/hare krishna/krishna krishna/hare hare/ hare rima/hare rama/rama rama/hare hare.

MR. WEINGLASS: Now, directing your attention to Monday night, that is August 26th, in the evening, where were you?

THE WITNESS: I was by a barricade that was set up, a pile of trash cans and police barricades, wooden horses, I believe. There were a lot of young kids, some black, some white, shouting and beating on the tin barrels, making a fearsome noise.

MR. WEINGLASS: What did you do after you got there?

THE WITNESS: Started chanting "Om." For a while I was joined in the chant by a lot of young people who were there until the chant encompassed most of the people by the barricade, and we raised a huge loud sustained series of "Oms" into the air loud enough to include everybody. Just as it reached, like, a great unison crescendo, all of a sudden a police car came rolling down into the group, right into the center of the group where I was standing, and with a lot of crashing and tinkling sound of glass, and broke up the chanting, broke up the unison and the physical—-everybody was holding on to each other physically—broke up that physical community that had been built and broke up the sound chant that had been built. I moved back. There was a crash of glass.[26]

## Back to Pooh

A dog whimpers and twitches in its sleep. The wind hums through the trees and the river has a humming, cruising sound that never stops as it runs over the rapids when I go upstate to the land without traffic or the shrieker. And then there's the pretty well continuous ringing in my ears, the ur-hum where insides meets outside in the one great hum of the great bumble bee.

Inoculating himself against the nostalgia of childhood, Walter Benjamin wrote how the hunchback from nursery rhymes who plagued him as a child, making him a perpetual loser, preceded him everywhere he went. You didn't see him but he always saw you. Under his gaze everything receded—the garden, the bench, his room—it was if they grew a hump. "When I go into my little room/ To have my little sweet,/ I find a little hunchback there/ Has eaten half the treat." But he has long since abdicated, wrote Benjamin, even though "his voice, like the hum of the gas burner, whispers to me over the threshold of the century: "Dear little child, I beg of you/ Pray for the little hunchback too."[27]

Yet did he really abdicate? Does not the humming implicate screaming? What else was the Angel of History but this same hum, this same hunchback, eyes staring, mouth open, and wings spread, staring at the wreckage piled at his feet, the feet of history?

Forty years ago a poet of the people found a very different relation to history, deflecting the standard revolutionary wisdom of the West with his call not to arms but to O-m-ms. At once profound and open, a Winnie-the-Pooh character if ever there was one, Allen Ginsberg updated that philosophy of history in which Walter Benjamin speaks of "chips of Messianic time," referring to what can happen when something from the traumatic past is suddenly brought into the present such that another world seems possible.

Bees of the world unite. You have nothing to lose but your chains.

---

26. "Testimony of Allen Ginsberg," law.umkc.edu/facultyprojects/trials/Chicago7trial/testimonyofallenginsberg (Chicago 7 Trail homepage).

27. Walter Benjamin, *Berlin Childhood around 1900* (Cambridge, MA: Belknap Press of Harvard University Press, 2006), 121–22.

# Excelente Zona Social

This was written for the twenty-fifth anniversary of the publication of the book *Writing Culture: The Poetics and Politics of Ethnography*, edited by James Clifford and George Marcus.

> In July of 2011 I spent two days in a camp of peasants being forced off their lands in the swamps of northern Colombia where the Magdalena River spills out across the lowlands before entering the Caribbean. The land is flooded twice a year and I was there as the waters were subsiding, accompanied by Juan Felipe García, a professor of law in Bogotá, Pablo Gómez, his assistant who kept track of our expenses, and Lily Hibberd, an Australian artist who had never been to Latin America. On the first night of our return trip we stayed at a hotel in the para- militarized town of Agua Chica called Don Pepe's Posada, located, according to its sign, in an excelente zona social.

Jimmy has it worked out. Just as the ancient city of Alexandria was to the poet Constantine Cavafy, so Bogotá is to him, the wellspring of his fiction and nonfiction, alike. Actually Jimmy lives in self-imposed exile, having grown up in New York City. He attended Columbia University in the sixties but dropped out searching for a more meaningful life, first in western Ireland, then Colombia where he found a home. So it seems fair to say he inhabits in his soul two cities. Me too, I want to say, but my other city is not Bogotá but an agribusiness town called Puerto Tejada and beyond that a territory extending over southwest Colombia; from the mangrove swamps of the Pacific over the *cordilleras* to the foothills of the Andes falling into the Amazon. I guess we could with unseemly immodesty continue; Faulkner and Yoknapatawphaw county, Hardy and Wessex, García Márquez and Macondo, George Elliot and Middlemarch. . . . But these are fictional names for real places whereas for Jimmy and me, while the place is real enough, our writing a little less so.

Cavafy has a poem he wrote in 1896 called *Confusion*:

My soul, in the middle of the night,
is confused and paralyzed. Outside:
its life comes into being outside itself
And it awaits the improbable dawn.
And I await, am worn down, and am bored,
even I who am in it or with it.

On a balcony on a brand new high-rise facing the blackness of the mountains sheer in our face, an elegant young law professor, whiskey in hand, expounds on the origin of the new constitution of 1991. But each story requires another to explain it. We get locked into a cats' cradle of interconnecting but incomplete stories in a sort of hysteria of history with the native being egged on by the outsider (me) for the sake of the newcomer (Lily). It is cold under these stars with all this glass and shiny steel around us of the New City built on top of pokey red-brick two-story bourgeois homes with Tudor facades considered elegant in their day before becoming abortion clinics and brothels and then Xerox shops, and rapid delivery mail stores. Twenty-two stories below thread the lights of traffic like a string of pearls. The new constitution came about largely because of the student movement, he says, a bunch of eighteen-year-olds, many from the Jesuit university, *La Javeriana*. The M-19 guerrilla joined the students later, he assures us, as did the FARC guerrilla who were ready to sign on but the government couldn't tolerate that so bombed them from the air. (The government needs the guerrilla, he says, needs an enemy within, the anti-Christ. This is in effect their strongest ally, better than the US.) The students had a stimulating conversation with the leader of the M-19 when he signed on. What was meant to be a five-minute formality extended to three hours of animated conversation. Next day he was assassinated. The stars are fiercely alive at this height although technically dead but we don't recognize that because it takes so long for their light to reach us through this cold air. A burly ex-M-19 *guerrillero* looks on but does not say much. He seems strangely absent, now a non-being on the wrong side of history, out of place in these shimmering towers without a story of his own. He belongs to the past where history becomes someone else's story.

Faulkner not only told stories but told language. He wrote with the limitless power of the language questioning itself in what in the 1980s I came to call in Colombia "multiple realities" whereby each person sees the same thing differently. One book, *As I Lay Dying*, has separate chapters for each member of the dead woman's family talking to themselves. Susan Willis told me Faulkner wanted the book printed such that each person's chapter would have a separate color. In my town in Colombia this multiplicity of overlapping realities became apparent to me under three conditions: (1) stories of origins of local saints, (2) stories as to how corpses on roads into town got to be there, and (3) most importantly, when I started to write about these things.

Sometimes when you write field notes time stands still and an image takes its place. On occasions the image is tactile. Just about the softest thing I ever touched was powdered coca leaf prepared by the Huitoto Indians of the Igaraparaná and Caraparaná affluents of the Putumayo River which itself runs into the Amazon. Jimmy had some in the fridge but said it was a little too old to *mambear*, meaning put into your mouth with lime and hold it there a while like a wad of tobacco. It's good for writing, he says, but makes you want to chain-smoke cigarettes. But hey! Anything for writing. His kid Rafael made a Nobel Prize for Literature certificate and hung it on the wall above his desk. Feeling the coca powder with my finger and thumb was beautiful, like the softest velvet, resonating with the subtlety of its color between light green and gray, like stardust, if you know what I mean. Dust, that's for sure, the dust so fine it's where substance gives way to immateriality.

Juan Álvaro, who teaches anthropology in a university deep in the Amazon, has a plastic bag with much fresher coca leaf powder than Jimmy's and uses it quite a bit. He hangs out with Huitotos and speaks their language. I have memories of him in his glassed-in somewhat makeshift penthouse in downtown Bogotá where he spends half his time surrounded by all manner of exotic plants such as a giant San Pedro cactus from northern Peru. What an anomaly! A desert cactus on the roof outside in drizzly Bogotá at eight thousand feet. His house is like a watchtower, tilting to one side with a spiral staircase inside and a loopy old dog whose claws make frantic noises scratching the wooden steps as she clambers up and down afraid of missing the excitement. Modernized apartments for hipsters stare at us from across the way as Juan Álvaro sucks his finger dipped in concentrated tobacco juice at the same time as he chews on the coca powder, like Huitoto men do when they gather in a circle to talk and tell stories. He keeps the tobacco juice in a small bottle shaped like a penis. He hands it around. The juice is extremely strong, toxic is what I want to say, roaring like fire through your innermost being, but his voice is as soft as the coca powder. The ink black tobacco juice drips down either side of his mouth as he speaks, giving him black fangs. His mouth—organ of speech—is transformed and transforming, adding to that chain of storytelling which has the power to change the world, storytelling being the art of penultimatcity—the one permanently before the last.

Many years back when I was reading Roger Casement's 1910 field reports to Sir Edward Grey of the British Foreign Office concerning the atrocities committed by the Amazon Rubber Company against the Huitoto Indians, I asked two Colombian anthropologists what Huitotos, with whom they worked, recalled of those atrocities?

Why do you want to know about this? they were told. Only sorcerers want such stories. With them they kill.

In our age, when in a mere three decades it has become fashionable to enthuse about storytelling and the rediscovery of narration—in advertising and politics, in law and talk radio, in medicine and social science, in psychotherapy and truth and reconciliation commissions—it can be a shock to be told to back off by an older tradition of storytelling more keenly beholden to the powers therein.

It is as if experience is something to be weighed, not consumed.

In thinking about storytelling as an outgrowth of place, it is helpful to remember Walter Benjamin's suggestion that the origin of storytelling lies in the encounter between the traveler and those who stay at home. He emphasizes the role played by the seafarer and the artisan as wandering journeyman, but in our day and age is it not the displaced person and illegal immigrant who assume that role? In which case, place assumes the status of a phantom limb.

Powered by a small outboard engine our canoe—known as a "Johnson," referring to the first outboard motors here and pronounced "yonson"—pushes through brilliantly colored flowers—white, purple, and a bloody red—that spread like a floating carpet over the surface of the water. Great

white herons stand solitary on one leg in haughty disdain, flying off slowly at the last minute as we approach, stretching open their enormous white wings like fans against the bright green. They are strange these birds, that's for sure, one moment clumsy, the next moment extremely graceful, catching themselves as they seem to fall. Black ducks skid across the clear brown waters. After the flooding every six months there are plenty of fish in the swamps. *Mojarra.* I got to know the taste well. This enormous area of wilderness, of swamps that go on forever, is one of the world's least known paradises. What a fate to plant it in African Palm row after row for diesel fuel.

My law professor friend Juan Felipe García has been here in these swamps of northern Colombia fifteen times, sometimes accompanied by his law professor colleague Roberto Vidal. It takes two days of travel from Bogotá by plane, bus, taxi, launch, motorbike, and "Johnson." They work pro bono. On either side of Juan Felipe's office in the Jesuit university in Bogotá are law professors who work as paid consultants for large landowners. "It was always the Jesuit way," he explains with perhaps too much cynicism, "To help the poor while at the same time sustain the system." His mission is to get the land restored to the 120 families displaced initially by a drug lord, Jesús Emilio Escobar, a relative of the infamous Pablo, laundering money and growing coca. In the early 1990s in its usually desultory efforts to curtail drugs, the state claimed the land which thereafter lay abandoned and the peasants reoccupied it, claiming it should revert to them. Paramilitaries from the *Bloque Central* forced them off in 2003. But the peasants returned. Then Jesús Emilio returned in 2006 with an army and forced them off again. One of the wealthiest men in Santa Marta—site of Joseph Conrad's novel *Nostromo*, located north on the Caribbean coast—bought the rights to plant African Palm from Jesús Emilio in 2006, and since then African Palm cultivation has proceeded apace, alongside the plantations of the sons of ex-president Uribe who had the Medal of Freedom bestowed on his scrawny chest by George W. Bush for his fight against terrorists even though he is widely considered a major force behind the various paramilitaries that swarm throughout rural Colombia.

A few months before our visit, the regular police forced the peasants off once more. It took at least an hour for the ring of sixty police dressed in their medieval-looking riot gear to advance slowly, step by step, toward the hacienda building the peasants were occupying so as to make them leave. Is it not exceedingly strange to see such police in the swamps, just as it is now strange to have the peasants hand me their photographs of this event and be propelled back in time to this decisive moment. Both the police and the photographs compress time, abutting the prehistoric life of the swamp with the leviathan of the modern state glistening in plastic armor. Step by step like a yoga exercise in slow motion, another theater performance.

Speaking of theater, the land in question presents a dramatic cross section through history. It is largely forested where not planted in African Palm or given over to slash and burn peasant cultivation which has been on the wane the past ten years on account of the violence. It measures some three thousand hectares, and tends to be higher than its surroundings, making it better for cultivation. The hacienda building is the symbolic center of the violence which is why the peasants built their tent village right by it. Both rest upon a raised field about eighty centimeters high, said to have been built by the Indians who existed here until the peasants arrived in the 1930s from San Martín de Loba.

The peasants rarely held title to the land they farmed and if bought out by the rich it was not the land but the so-called *mejoras*, or improvements that were sold. You have to ask yourself first why the peasants did not acquire title, and, second, see in this not merely neglect, ignorance, or lack

of means to deal with bureaucracy or pay a lawyer and a surveyor, but also a clash of civilizations, one based on writing and the state, the other based on knowing the land and claiming it through working it.

Nevertheless Juan Felipe and Roberto have won the first legal battle. The case went to the top court in the land, the Constitutional Court, which held that the use of riot police to force the peasants off the land, for the third time in the past thirty years, was illegal. Now the decision as to whom can claim ownership rests with a government-appointed land reform institute until recently stacked with the paramilitary allies of ex- president Uribe, still a power to be reckoned with.

In the village of Buenos Aires on the river before I got to this camp, I had seen a video of a confrontation showing the dark-skinned lawyer of the *palmeros*—as the African palm plantation owners are known—with his bodyguards berating the peasants with all manner of high-flown legalese to make them leave. I was with Misael's family. Every now and then someone watching the video with me would make a comment. The past is not what it used to be, not with videos replaying history.

A neurologically disturbed mute woman, perhaps like this since birth, aged about eighteen, I thought, but turns out to be more like forty, would walk back and forth and occasionally come in and glance at the video or stare at me for several minutes at a time, wringing her twisted hands, her arms knotted with tension. She would sit and lie in a sand pit made for her, carving ephemeral forms and sculptures with a broken machete. Outside on the one street constituting the village, two small girls aged ten or so were making castles in the sand decorated with flowers. I don't see any toys, just this sand art with its fantastic, utopian promise.

A small dreamy boy living in the same household was nursing a broken arm set in plaster. He had been taken by "Johnson" three hours downstream to the town of El Banco and from there by ambulance to Santa Marta many hours away. An epic journey on account of there being no medical services. His mother took off a few years ago and his grandparents and aunt take loving care of him and his sister. It may sound soppy, but I have rarely seen such love, patience, and good humor.

Like a scene out of *One Hundred Years of Solitude*, the peasants first came to this region with their burros and dug-out canoes in the 1930s exploring the tributaries and winding rivulets of the Magdalena. Living in these vast swamps of mud and floating plants, they practiced an amphibious mode of life adapted to the rise and fall of the waters as had the Indians before them,, so I am told, drifted away to the mountains and valleys of the Sierra Nevada to join other Indians such as the Arahuacos living there.

In his 1978 three-volume study, *Historia doble de la costa*, Orlando Fals-Borda coins the term *amphibious mode of productio* for this mode of life, providing an experimental historical ethnography which, amphibious in its own right, puts travelers' tales, anecdotal observations, and phenomenological impressions on the left-hand page, and social sciencey stuff on the right-hand page—hence *historia doble*. It is incredible how boring if not pretentious and quite silly the right-hand side has become, testimony to the short half-life of "theory," while the left-hand side seems to increase its power over time like a good wine.

Something else stands out with this amphibiousness and that is the role in world history of people who live in swamps and adapt to the changing water levels at the mouths of great rivers. Much of world history includes such people, just as much of world history can be summed up as the drainage of vast wetlands and the building of dykes against rivers and oceans. While a romanticized *nomadism* as a trope has caught the eye of many Deleuzians, the swamp people of world history seem predestined to invisibility. None of that wild movement on swift horses across the deserts and plains. Just vicious mosquitoes, sludge and wetness and kids making sandcastles on the sandy streets of riverbank villages in the dry season, awash with water and glue-like mud in the wet.

Juan Felipe brings out maps bought at the Colombian Geographical Institute Codazzi. He wants the peasants to check these official maps and annotate them with their own historical referents drawn from memory. Second, he wants to discuss a map showing how the territory could be used if they were able to get it back, complete with waterways for transport, a swamp reserve of forest, replanting trees along with land set aside for private plots of rice, yucca, and cattle. The peasants call him "profe" as in professor, a term of endearment and respect all over Colombia.

Everyone but the children gather. Efraín Alvear starts a prayer. I am surprised by this. The only religious gatherings I know in Colombia are those administered by the catholic priest, evangelical pastors, or Indian shamans. Yet Efraín does sound like a pastor, except he is so gentle and grounded

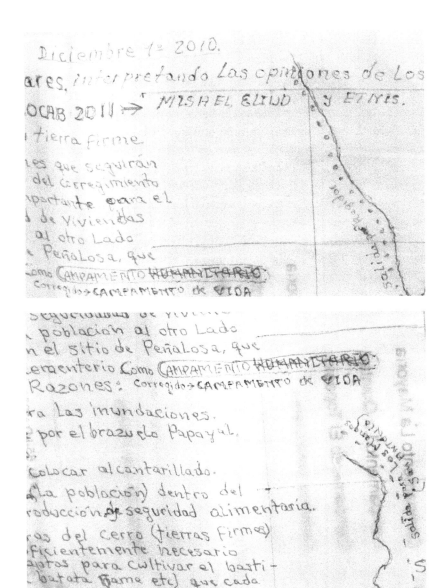

in the political situation at hand. This group prayer seems to me a "basic" religious impulse drawing on an overwhelming sense of exile, injustice, and solidarity. (Later on he tells me that he did actually train three years in a college for evangelists but found he was emotionally unable to accept this as his vocation.)

It is early morning and still cool. "We have to create a new language," says Juan Felipe. "The *palmeros* have theirs, and we need to show the world an alternate model." Then he asks, "Who recalls the founding of the village of Buenos Aires?" A man steps forth, puts his elbows on the table while standing, and starts a lengthy genealogy. Efraín Alvear writes it down. The witness has his back to the audience and is speaking very softly. Then another elderly man lists all the houses, one by one. It seems tedious to me but there are guffaws and rippling mirth. Misael asks four elderly men to name the houses in the *calle atras*, the smaller street in their tiny village by the river. We are off on a journey through time, threading names and events onto a new map.

Aged around sixty, Efraín Alvear finds it hard to walk due to an injection in his buttocks when he was a kid that damaged the sciatic nerve. In a physically taxing world you woud think this is a huge problem but he somehow compensates by being the scribe of this little community, by his kindness and prodigious intelligence, and by the generosity of others who hold him in great esteem. He keeps a daily journal and has drawn his own map.

What did he do before the troubles started, I wonder, when perhaps a chronicler was not necessary, and why does he do this? I see one entry in the journal which begins with "today was a day full of promise."

His map accentuates the cemetery, the crops, and the "beaches" which I guess are the fertile levees along the rivers which, if memory serves me right, are like common lands and cannot be alienated. (Later I learn this refers to the ponds that dry out after the six monthly floods.) Efrain's map is as much text as drawing, more a mimesis than an abstract diagram in that it strives to bring out the use, meaning, history, and dream future of land and settlements. His map is messy—a work in progress that will always be a work in progress—and differs a great deal from the state's maps on account of its abundance of information and something harder to define, endless curiosity and love or at least intimacy which you see again and again in the intensity with which he and others pour over the maps, their homemade ones as well as what Juan Felipe brings from the nation's capital. The maps become symbols and substitutes for the land, something we can reduce to a few square inches and manipulate like magicians with their spells.

They are placed on a crude table chest-high, and the men cluster around this, then drift away after an hour, leaving the discussion to a handful of elders and the scribe. There are no women, other than those young and

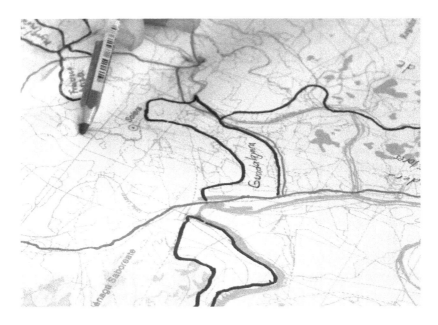

middle-aged women tending great tubs of fish and manioc. (When the ponds recede after the flood the ponds are full of fish.) As the sun gathers force, excitement around the maps wanes. Heat rises under the black plastic ceiling. It is hard to imagine a more awful combination than black plastic and this humid heat.

Two adorable four-year-old twin boys are playing on their hands and knees in the sand to one side of us making their own sort of map, an imaginary road system for their cars, two old cans of tuna.

Their road system reminds me of the sand sculptures the kids make back in the village (where there are no cars at all, but plenty of mules, donkeys, and motorbikes). And why tuna? Aren't there loads of fish here? The label on their underpants is visible. It says "American Rangers." Kids, pigs, and dogs roll around together in spiraling confusion. The pond in front of us is covered with thick green slime and at night there are so many frogs croaking you can barely think.

Much of the week the peasants live in their village on the edge of a tributary called the *brazuelo de Papayal* (such a beautiful name, with *Papayal* meaning grove of papaya trees) which runs into the Magdalena River. Painted in bright colors, the houses are of adobe or cement blocks. The trunks of the trees along the street are also painted in colors matching the houses. The roofs are of corrugated iron or dense thatch, and all houses

Pablo & Efraín
Pouring over
the map—
under black
plastic ceiling

Placed
under the
thatch.

(1)

PABLO

Don EFRAÍN

See
foto
100

Amazing how much (? infinite)
knowledge he has & the entire
region—who owns what, the machos, etc
history & land holdings; at one point he calls
bait to compare a point.

have a *ramada* of thatch providing relief from the stifling heat. Many of the houses have septic tanks and all have electricity from the faraway town of El Banco. There is erratic cell phone coverage, money seems non-existent, and the two or three stores are pitiful.

So as to keep their moral if not legal right to territory alive, the peasants active in the land claim built this tent city a one-hour walk away from the village (at their speed of walking). They have divided themselves into three groups such that every two to three days a new group stays in the tent city and the others remain in the village by the river. I see a young man and woman walking back through the swamp carrying their belongings in a large plastic trash bag. No L. L. Bean or North Face wilderness gear for the inhabitants of this wilderness, as wild physically as it is politically.

There is a constant fear of physical attack. Stories of confrontations abound. At sunset the peasants form a guard along the fence dividing this black plastic encampment from the hacienda building in which three or four employees of the African Palm growers reside. They take shifts as night watchmen.

I look for a place to take a shit and find there is no latrine and am pointed vaguely to a field full of young African palms, like fat pineapples, in neat rows. It is hard to walk anywhere because of the mud. (Walking to this encampment the day before I had to get hauled out when my calf-high rubber boots stuck in the mud.) It is satisfying—indeed a sublimely revolutionary

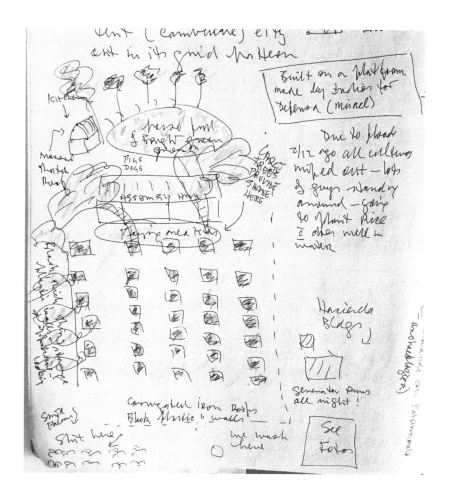

act, is it not?—to shit in the palm field of the bio-fuelers (i.e., the *palmeros*) as the sun sets in sublime sheets of reds and yellows over the ridge.

I am told that a guard made of Paéz or Guambiano Indians all the way from Cauca in the south of the country have been here armed with nothing but their staves to provide support and there is a group of Swiss who do the same thing, "bearing witness," as they say. I joke, "Why not have three German sanitary engineers here for a week to make some toilets?"

Looking out over the squat African Palms I sit with six of the younger men sprawled on a piece of *palmero* farm equipment quietly watching the colors in the sky. The mood has shifted from the practical to the poetic, like what happens shitting in the palm field. Alexander is here, aged twenty-nine. I call him "the poet." He has no job, he says, and has never worked. His

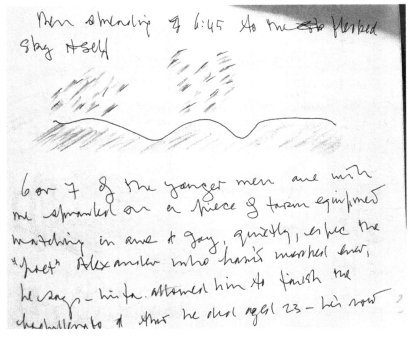

father allowed him to finish high school and that he did aged twenty-three. How can I understand his not working? The valleys in the far-off ridges of what I take to be the *Serranía* of San Lucas fill with a golden haze while along the hilltops the gold forms a thin ribbon running along the bluish green of the hills.

Not a word passes between us. Triggered by the ascending price for gold, the *serranía* is now subject to a gold rush with miners using mercury which gets into the waterways here, a man told me. But not much, he adds. The *serranía* is also the home for the guerrilla, first the ELN and now the FARC. All that is there, on the horizon. And now the sky is flecked, purple and red.

Meanwhile the "enemy," as they are called, the employees of the *palmeros'* hacienda, switch on an electric generator which makes a terrible racket. Their lights will glare the night long making our sleep difficult. It is all so strange, our camp and their camp, cheek by jowl, our camp of black plastic sheeting, theirs a solid-looking hacienda building with a menacing back hoe standing guard as its angel of death. It gets stranger still, as two of the men hired by the hacienda are accomplished accordion players who join us on our return canoe trip, complete with *tambor* and aguardiente. Best of pals.

As the darkness gathers I decide to copy Lily, who has been accompanied by a group of women to a bathing place by the side of the African Palms. I walk through the mud with a flashlight accompanied by a one-armed young man named José who appears out of nowhere. We reach a small pond the size of a bathtub four feet down a muddy slope which has crude, slippery steps, set into it. He holds my hand in his good hand. I slip as I descend. His grip is firm and comforting. It is pitch black. He wears swimming trunks and nothing else. With infinite care I take off one sandal, then another. Then he hands me a container for scooping up the muddy water so as to douse myself. Out of fear of offending him I do not strip completely naked. Then like a crab I make my way up again. This one-armed gentle man who appeared out of nowhere has become my guardian angel.

Only some 30 percent of the people in the village are behind this movement to claim territory, Juan Felipe tells me, and they are mainly middle-aged and elderly. What's up with the rest? I wonder, then think of other places in Colombia that I know of, and then the world at large since it seems that young people pretty much all over have turned their back on agriculture.

Coming to this place in the "Johnson" took about five hours as the motor refused to start. The current was with us. We drifted as the *motorista*, sweating profusely, tried again and again to yank the motor into action. Up front sang the balladeer. He answers my questions with songs of violence and violation, of betrayal by the "black Judas" who swore a deposition in the state capital, Cartagena, that the peasants had not been forcibly displaced, this same Judas who now has a salaried job with the African Palm owners. Sung in a high falsetto, like Woody Guthrie, these *vallenatos* sung to a Hohner accordion (always a Hohner; always from the same town in

Germany), are famous throughout the north of Colombia as songs of protest as much as of love and betrayal. The hours pass. The sun beats down. The great white heron spread its wings like the swan enrapturing Leda as we float downstream through the floating verdure. He sings of the paramilitaries and the terror they create, chopping up bodies and heaving them into the river upon which we float with its vivid flowers. He stops singing for a moment and tells me how, when swimming in this river, he felt an arm and then a hand clutching at his throat. I don't believe a word of it.

(Did I hear right?) Then he starts singing again. We stop to fix the motor at a bunch of houses made of packed mud. A stout schoolteacher joins us. Her blood pressure fell suddenly and she was taken here for medical attention. The conversation turns once again to the violent and bizarre, stage two, you might say, of an ongoing rhapsody as the canoe, now moving briskly, raises a fine spray in a glistening arc overhead.

What would the Huitotos say about this? Are we like the sorcerers, gathering tales of atrocity with which to empower ourselves? What is our humanism, really? Why do we gorge ourselves on these stories? What of Walter Benjamin and his claim—at once dubious and convincing—that storytelling is a dead art, especially in times of war?

Why do they put the bodies in the river? I ask. Because they won't let them be buried, she replies. This takes time to sink in. Life is important, but I get the feeling burial is more so. Don't Vico and Bataille see in burial the first sign of culture, the first sign of being human? Therefore, not to bury and, even more, to refuse burial, strikes at the heart of culture and at what separates the human from the inhumane. Yet is not the inhumane brimful of sacred power too, albeit the power of evil and "the negative sacred"?

A human body is the ultimate territory and a chopped-up corpse adrift in the river is the absolute denial of such territory, the deepest possible exile of the soul. Thus does deterritorialization achieve its most definitive state of non-being. Could this be why the counterforce claiming territory as mythical power is now every day ascendant in Colombia, after two decades of paramilitary violence aimed at dismembering both land and body?

The territory of the body, that is the corpse, is not lost on Vladimir either. He is an ex-paramilitary who deserted through fear and, of all things, because he hated oatmeal for breakfast. I can't stand *avena*, he explains. He was recruited in Caicedonia in the Valle and was taken to a training school lasting forty-five days near Líbano in Tolima. He spares no detail. They cut open the body of a guerrilla fighter, stuffed it with cocaine, and drove it to Medellín in a hearse. Another time he was working on a dairy farm in Antioquia and had to walk somewhere at three in the morning. He saw headlights of three pick-up trucks in a stream and then he saw two bodies, one being cut to pieces with a belt around the man's mouth to stop him screaming. The other man was dead and his body was being packed with what most likely was cocaine. Vladimir crept past. Walking up the hill he heard the sound of a motorbike of *alto cylindrage* coming down the hill, *muy suave*. The driver stopped and asked him if he'd seen anything down at the stream? Oh! No! He replied. Are you sure? Of course I'm sure.

Some questions: Why does he tell us this, his fellow passangers cleaving the waters of the *Brazuelo de Papayal* in sheets of spray, careening without a care in the world? And is it not a little strange that a paramilitary—albeit a self-declared ex-paramilitary—should be so ready to reveal his past like this? Even if it's not true, or partly untrue, it is still strange, All for the sake of a good story, you say, a cornucopia of such, his "return gift" to the society he has despoiled, his "payment" instead of a jail sentence, or worse? When you bear in mind also that the whole category of an "ex-para" is clouded with suspicion, that there is no such thing as an *ex* in these matters, then perhaps we can see him as the Great Performer trying to charm his way to repentance?

The tent city, like the hacienda building next to it, is built on a platform of packed earth about three hundred feet square and thirty inches high so as to resist floodwaters. I am told it was used for dwellings and cultivation in pre-Colombian times. It is marvelous to be on this platform continuing a tradition one thousand or more years old, yet so modest, so beautifully "low-tech." Misael brings out two stone cutting tools he has discovered there about five inches long. They are surprisingly heavy. It is exceedingly strange to live in this gridwork of black plastic homes erected on pre-Colombian earthworks with heavy stone tools scattered around. I recommend it to anyone in search of a territory in this modern age; the permanence of the earth below, itself an indigenous artifact, sustaining the impermanence of the glistening plastic shelters above.

It must seem frivolous if I pause to consider my fieldwork notebook as "territory" in this sense too, but then is not the notebook the means of production of the anthropologist as much as the watery land is to the peasant cultivator?

Might this be even more so as regards the phantom land that, now displaced, is filled with turbulence and hope of redemption every bit as glowing as those ridges of the *Serranía de San Lucas* with the sky now flecking purple and red? And just as land as territory is a lot more than means to an end, can we not say the same about the fieldwork notebook which, quickly, becomes an end in itself, a veritable fetish cherished as a work not only of documentation but of secret signs and occult art as well?

I had been thinking along these lines for several years ever since I published in 2003 a diary of two weeks in a Colombian town in 2001 taken over by hired killers identified by many as paramilitaries. In reorganizing my diary of those two weeks so as to create a book, I realized that an ethnographic notebook or diary can mean very different things and be written in a great variety of ways such that in the final analysis the very notions of the Self to whom one purportedly writes dissolves no less than the meaning of writing and representation along with—and this is crucial—the events and thoughts depicted. A diary thereby matches the fragmented and multiple nature of social reality, analogous to the terror I experienced in Colombia. I came across a note in my notebook of this trip into the swamp that read: "These trips become as much a trip into one's past and into one's being as they are journeys into the unknown. What effort must be expended by travelers and anthropologists to ignore this."

Aspects of this came to light for me when a student at CalArts directed me many years back toward Brion Gysin and William Burrough's 1961 scrapbooks based on what Gysin called the cut-up principle juxtaposing images with slabs of text so as to transform one's understanding of reality. With that I got to thinking about fieldwork notebooks with their more or less randomized observations, meta-observations, insights, afterthoughts, and images, as having the potential—at least the potential—to be considered as modernist art objects with magical properties like fetishes and talismans capable of acting on the world.

Here Walter Benjamin's use of what he called "thought-images" or *Denkbilden* combining ethnography with dreams and fiction come forcibly to mind as well. He had already tried something like this in his small book of 1928 entitled *One Way Street*, but the trips to what he thought of as an "outpost" of Europe, namely Ibiza, brought this to a head.

All this suggests—like Clifford and Marcus's *Writing Culture* and, before that Marcus and Fischer's *Anthropology as Cultural Critique*—that fieldwork is inseparable from writingwork and that the notebook with its sketches and forays has its own riches of form and content that cannot and should not be seen as mere stepping stones to the polished end-product of a book or article.

If there is something absurd if not insulting about ethnographic writing based on two days and two nights, with some additional material based on notes the days prior, is it not also the case that first impressions are generally more vivid than subsequent ones? What are we to make of this? And what of the responsibility to oneself as much as one's hosts to put something of those impressions out into the world, together with the responsibility to get it right?

To this it should be noted that what happens when notes are "written up" is that what I call "afterthoughts" kick in. By afterthoughts I mean secondary elaborations that arise on top of the original notes, photographs, and drawings. Through stops, starts, and sudden swerves, the original is pulled into a wider and wilder landscape. To reread and to rewrite is to tug at the memories buried therein as well as engage with the gaps, questions, connections, conundrums, and big ideas that lie latent and in turn generate more of the same. In essence my talk today is exactly that, an afterthought that has, with the passage of three weeks, slipped away from its moorings while preserving the imprimatur if not the character of the original.

I feel impelled to ask, therefore, if anthropology has sold itself short in conforming to the idea that its main vehicle of expression is an academic book or journal article? This is not a plea for exact reproduction of the fieldwork notebook but rather a plea for following its furtive forms and mix of private and public in what can only be called, as in cinema, a "dissolve" or "fade out" that captures ephemeral realities, the check and bluff of life.

At the end of the day one is left with an image of a cocaine-rich man with a checkbook and a lawyer and a bunch of thugs turning up one day in the swamp saying it's all his now, recorded in the deed book of properties in far-off Cartagena, capital of the state, a walled port built over two centuries by slaves from Africa baptized by the Jesuits in the cathedral of San Pedro Claver. Other rich men follow in order to plant African Palm for diesel fuel to power the endless stream of trucks running north and south night and day along the highway connecting Barranquilla, the port at the mouth of the Magdalena, with the interior. At night the trucks are beautifully illuminated with row after row of twinkling lights emitting much mystery. The landlords build roads through the swamp that interrupt the flow of waters. They say there are no peasants, merely landless laborers. They say there is no war, merely a bunch of bandits making trouble. A songster sings of feeling a chopped-off arm and hand clutching at his throat while he swims in the river. The more swamp the men with the checkbooks take, however, the more they provoke an idea of territory belonging to those who work it, territory meaning a place with a history that, depending on your outlook, is evidenced by Indian earthworks going way back in time, or black plastic villages where now the map is being rewritten as memory opens like the fan of the great white wings of the heron against the green of the swamp.

## Coda

In February 2013, some eighteen months after our visit, Juan Felipe tells me that the land reform institute has decided to expropriate the African Palm growers and that as a result the latter have gone to the Council of State which will take between two to eight years to hand down what will be the final decision. Meanwhile the peasants keep on cultivating despite continuous threats by the paramilitaries employed by the palm growers. Although aware of this situation, the national attorney general's office does nothing.

# I'm So Angry I Made a Sign

*A Note on Form*

I have inserted the signs in Zuccotti Park as set-apart quotations in the center of the page.

And sometimes I have also inserted quotes from texts by philosophers, poets, and other people worth listening to. They, too, look like signs. I don't think you will confuse them, but it's better if you do.

*A Note on Strategy*

Nietzsche says somewhere that a historian has to create a text equal to what is being written about. This would seem especially compelling when it comes to Occupy Wall Street.

> And as concerns history, or at least its retelling, coming back to this text
> of mine three years after it was written is like visiting a strange and fabu-
> lous land. I imagine it will be the same for you.
> Wall St is everywhere
> therefore we have to occupy everywhere

## 11:00 p.m., October 13, 2011

On my way downtown to Occupy Wall Street, Zuccotti Park, New York City. Flustered and excited. E-mails coming in from Yesenia, and from Michelle and Alex in my sorcery and magic class at Columbia. They should

Thanks to Nancy Goldring for many of the photographs that appear here. Thanks to Danny Alonso, Salomeya Sobko, Alex Afifi, and Michelle Rosales for their written observations, to Yesenia Baragan for always keeping me in the know, to Ayesha Adamo for good cheer, and to David Goldstein for his record of signs sent to me by Peter Lamborn Wilson.

be writing their weekly assignments for school. They are so far behind. But this is the night the mayor will attack. I stop by the bagel store to tell my Mexican friend about the drama unfolding downtown. He is counting money and is preoccupied. He has never heard of OWS and he tries to look interested. My canvas bag is stuffed with sleeping bags for Saa and myself. Long wait for the #1 train. Unbearable. Alex says rumors of police closing in at midnight. Danny Alonso, also in my sorcery class, once compared visiting Zuccotti Park—which he did all the time from day one—to the excitement of going to the movies and getting into the trance of that other reality. You get hooked, he later wrote. "I would be hypnotized and turned into someone else." In fact, many selves. A drumming self. A facilitator self. A hunting and gathering self roaming Manhattan for tarpaulins and food from dumpsters to bring the tribe, listening to stories "and healing from people who had come from all over to share in this moment." Many of these people had lost their jobs.

---

## Lost my job but found an occupation

---

You break through the screen, like Alice in Wonderland. And now you can't leave or do without it. Everything else seems fake and boring. So how do you write about it? In such circumstances of dissolving norms, effervescent atmosphere, invention and reinvention, what happens to the ethnographer's magic—as Malinowski called it—and that old standby of "participant observation?"

Is the (ethnographer's) magic strong enough?

In Malinowski's case the magic meant a great mimetic capacity to create scenes and give them color. More than that it meant combining the so-called scientific approach of a professionalizing anthropology with an intuitive grasp of what he called "the imponderabilia of everyday life" (both the natives' and his own), meaning the stuff that fell between the cracks of so-called structure, what Carlo Ginzburg calls "conjectural knowledge" based in millennia of hunting skill at reading signs and what Michael Polanyi calls "tacit knowing."[1] That sort of thing. As every mother knows.

Am I clear here? Let me try a different tack. That word "magic" as in "the ethnographer's magic"— it is a metaphor, right? But then what of the

1. Carlo Ginzburg, " Morelli, Freud, and Sherlck Holmes: Clues and Scientific Method," introduction byAnna Davin, in *History Workshop Journal* 9 (Spring 1980): 5–36; Michael Polanyi, *The Tacit Dimension* (Chicago: University of Chicago Press, 2009 [1966]).

Photograph by Nancy Goldring.

natives' magic? That is not so metaphoric but consists of "linguistic contagion," of words whispered into things such as plants to make them grow and be beautiful, into canoes to make them faster and safer, into the red of the betel nut juice to make it redder and one's skin glow, into herbs to be worn and burnt as love magic. What of this sort of magic? Does it occur in "the ethnographer's magic"?

What has our ethnographer really learned from the natives that he

Photograph by the author.

didn't know before? How many of us live like this, recycling the known? Whatever *Occupy* means, it means un-occupying that!

Am I being clear here? I don't think so, and I think this is the problem of writing surprise and writing strangeness, surely the dilemma and sine qua non of ethnography? As soon as you write surprise—or, rather, attempt to write it—it is as if the surprise has been made digestible so it is no longer surprising and no longer strange. Nietzsche urges restraint. Don't reduce the unknown to the known because that is a defensive gesture, afraid of difference and, moreover, such a reduction diverts attention away from how weird is the known which, in the case of *Occupy*, would truly miss the point. He pleads for patience, fair-mindedness, and gentleness with what is strange such that it will gradually present itself as a new and indescribable beauty that in turn teaches us how to love. That is our reward.[2]

To write about *Occupy* provides this in spades. The challenge of how to write surprise, think it, experience its bursting upon the scene of history, its inventiveness and charms, is its contribution to the human condition.

To "occupy ethnography" is to seize on the means and manner of representation as estranged. An exuberant style is not enough. That is why

2. Friedrich Nietzsche, *The Gay Science*, trans. Josefine Nauckhoff and Adrian Del Caro (Cambridge: Cambridge University Press, 2001), 186.

Photograph by Nancy Goldring.

I so much like the zombie-style bodies and faces of the sign holders who populate Zuccotti Park, graven images outside time, things speaking to things going one step better than Malinowski's magicians breathing words into things to as bring them to life, to new life.

Welcome to Hakim Bey's Temporary Autonomous Zone. I recall Paris, May 1968: people said they lived in that zone for months, didn't sleep, didn't need to. Out of nowhere a community forms, fueled by the unforeseen chance to fight back. Decades drift away. Decades of Fox News and Goldman

Photograph by Nancy Goldring.

Sachs. Decades of gutting what was left of the social contract. Decades in which kids came to think being a banker was sexy. When that happens, you *know* it's all over—or about to explode, as once again history throws a curveball. Once in a lifetime, the unpredictable occurs and reality gets redefined.

The most striking sign I have seen at Zuccotti Park over three months was a life-size painting of a man's striped tie on a white background. The tie was knotted to form a circle at the top like a hangman's noose. Wordless. Next to it was a sign with blotchy patches of white over some of the letters:

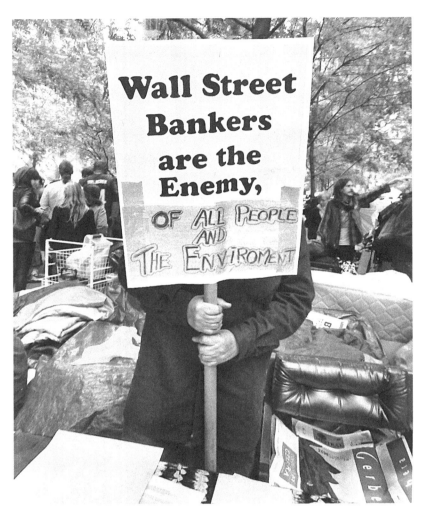

Photograph by Nancy Goldring.

They piss
on us and
call it
trickle down

America wakes up from the American Dream. "I've been waiting for this all my life," says Craig, who stayed with me overnight from California with naught but a backpack on his way to Zuccotti Park.

Photograph by the author.

## I awoke in a sweat
## from the American Dream

"At night we lie all together on the concrete," writes Alex, "a few sleeping, the rest talking in low voices, or reading next to the street lights, or cursing the constant sirens that we are certain the NYPD sends around the park at night just to keep us poorly rested and easily dominated, or looking through the thin canopy of leaves between the dark towers and the sky. The first morning we all agreed that we felt as if those buildings would fall in on us."

"Dear WB," she goes on, "maybe OWS is something like that awakening that is between sleep and consciousness. We are emerging from slumber but we are disoriented, stupored, caught between the dream logic of capitalism and the newly forming world."

"Dear WB." How blessed is that? She is writing code, of course—direct from the state of emergency and that other OWS of *One Way Street*. She is searching the zone of the dialectical image that Walter Benjamin envisaged as emerging from the dream sleep of capitalism that reactivated mythic powers. Just as one swims in the surreal zone of semisleep as harbinger of revolution, so does the epoch. Does the new security state understand and believe this too, along with Walter? Why else would they walk silently through the park at night, filming the sleepers?

**You must be asleep**
**to experience**
**the American Dream**

Salomeya put it a little differently. She has a theory, as usual. Working out of the sense of the body and magic she finds in Malinowski's discussions of clan and sub-clan solidarity and sorcery, she discerns a form of human bonding relevant to OWS that she calls "erotic materialism." It is a brilliant rereading of classical anthropology applied as much to Zuccotti Park as to aforesaid dream sleep mythology. (Now she tells me she suffers from being too abstract and goes on to add there's little she can do about it.)

But the lines get blurred. Solidarity gets tested. As time goes by, it is said that undercover police roam the park disguised as protesters. (Question: What does a protester look like?) It is said that homeless people are being directed by the police and shelters to go to Zuccotti Park in the hope that they will dilute and factionalize the occupation. The ideals of the radical hipsters from Brooklyn with their web-savvy culture are being tested like never before by these homeless men who seem uninterested in what the hipsters stand for, yet an abiding concern of OWS is homelessness. As time goes by—horror of horrors!—something like property and real estate interests surface. Someone quips that there is an Upper East Side section of tents in the park, and one hears muttering of gentrification, as if this utopic space is reproducing what it is against.

**We just bought real estate**
**in your mind**

It is said that there are rapes and stealing, and there certainly is stealing. Craig got all his stuff swiped after he left for half an hour to wash up in the bathroom of Trinity Church.

> ### I can hire one half of the
> ### working class
> ### to kill the other
> ### Jay Gould

I walk out of the subway at Fulton Street into the canyons of Wall Street, Fritz Lang's *Metropolis* based on his wife's script of soaring towers holding up a black sky heavy with rain clouds, workers in cages like moles—no speech in this movie (1927), only cryptic subtitles and madly gesticulating figures with pasty-white expressionist faces caught in frozen grimace. Police cars and vans are everywhere around the park and secreted in back alleys.

Down on the ground it is a war zone crackling with expectancy. But overhead, Freedom Tower, sheathed in mirrors, dwarfs everything, glistening with blue light. What did Benjamin say in "This Space for Rent" in *One Way Street*, that other OWS published as the fuse was being lit in Europe, in 1928, one year after *Metropolis*:

> ### What, in the end, makes advertisements superior to
> ### criticism? Not what the moving red neon says—
> ### but the fiery pool reflecting it in the asphalt

You take a deep breath when you get there and you can't breathe again until you leave. It is devastatingly spectacular and inhuman: the architecture of what Marx called M-M', meaning money making money, meaning finance capital, of which credit default swaps are the ultimate expression of the moneylenders whom Christ drove from the temple.

Is this what occupation of the park means—a moral movement against the exploitation of people not only by the moneylenders, but by the apparently neutral means of money doing it all on its own, meaning M-M'? Does the occupation occupy the magical energy of this fetish, and from this abundant source draw its energy?

Wall Street is forbiddingly allegorical. Fritz Lang provides a frightening topography of heaven and hell, of our Metropolis. But, closer to home, so did Diego Rivera in 1931, during the Great Depression, with his painting *Fondos Congelados* (Frozen Assets), showing the serene temples of Manhattan as an archaeological stratum atop a dimly lit subterranean morgue with corpses laid out in rows, supervised by a lonely guard. Perhaps they are not

Photograph by the author.

corpses, you say to yourself, but merely sleeping bodies. These are the "frozen assets": the unemployed laid out like corpses in prisonlike dwellings, bringing to mind the notion of capital as "congealed labor." It is a terrible picture. You could hear a pin drop.

But now, miraculously, with the occupation in full swing, the picture

Photograph by Nancy Goldring.

has come alive as the architecture of M-M′ loses its grip. We looked at each other eye-to-eye in those days, never quite knowing what the next enchanted moment would bring. We were bigger than the buildings, and instead of being physically compressed and mentally scripted, like the poor bastards in the offices all around us, we lived moment by moment, sparks flying from a knife grinder's wheel.

Even if Zuccotti was barren in winter as I wrote this, rarely did a day pass without mention in the media of OWS or the huge gap between the rich and the rest. The day I passed Zuccotti Park in mid-January, the mothers of girls in private schools of the Upper East Side, like Spence and Brearley, were reported in the *New York Times* as bemoaning the fact that, for the first time ever, their daughters had not gotten into Yale on early admission. Was that because of anger at the 1 percent? they wondered. That same day I passed a hole-in-the-wall restaurant uptown on Amsterdam Avenue and 102nd Street called Busters of New York. On a blackboard outside was displayed its menu:

---

**Wrap: "Occupy the Dream"**

---

Down the street from Zuccotti Park, the Museum of the American Indian. Right by the park, an African slave burial ground. How extraordinary! And right here in Zuccotti Park, many black protesters. But amid the hustle and bustle of the streets, does anyone notice that the center of the world's money—what makes this city so "global"—rests on top of skeletons of African slaves and ghosts of Indians, no doubt shaking wampum and featherwork. It is all so arty now, like Julie Mehretu's gorgeous five-million-dollar, eighty-foot-long mural adorning the glass-walled lobby of the new Goldman Sachs building along the Hudson, not so far away. They so want art, the 1 percent. Man does not live by bread alone. And art is a great—many say the greatest—investment in these troubled times. Three days before the occupation is forcibly ended by the baton-wielding NYPD, art shows its power:

---

**As Stocks Fall**
**Art Surges at a $315 Million Sale**

---

**Despite (or perhaps because of) the stock market's nearly**
**400 point plunge on Wednesday, collectors on Wednesday**
**night raced to put their available cash-and lots of it—**
**into art (*New York Times*, November 10, 2011)**

---

A little farther uptown, where prostitutes practiced their art and hoary truckers got laid, where the smell of rancid fat from the meat packing district used to be, now you have the lovely "high line" of swaying grasses along the abandoned railway tracks, the capstone of gentrification from which you can peer down into boutique stores and forget that Manhattan

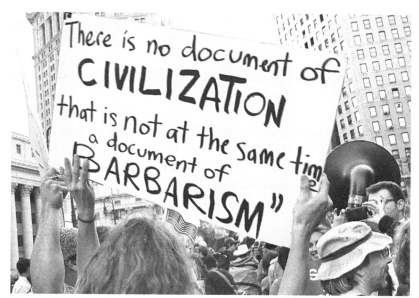

Photograph by the author.

has become unlivable for most people. What are all those smart people talking about in those chic restaurants? "Ultimately what Zuccotti Park is all about," Reinhold tells me (and he should know, urban planner that he is), "is real estate." What he means is that the occupation is testing the limits of monetarizing space. So what we have is

real estate
finance capital
art
and now OWS (another form of art)

Man does not live by bread alone. They so need art, the 1 percent. *But so does OWS.* This is not only a struggle about income disparity and corporate control of democracy. It is about the practice of art, too, including the art of being alive.

History congeals, then dissolves; and somehow art always ends up being art. When some OWS-inspired people dropped a banner inside the Museum of Modern Art in support of the art handlers locked out of Sotheby's, MOMA people quickly appropriated the banner as art.

History congeals, then dissolves. The chiseled stone of the older Wall

Street buildings gives way to mirrored buildings fighting free of history on postmodern wings. Money helps. Night and day, the crescendo of jackhammers obliterates time itself. Cranes lace the sky, adding new constellations. "All that is solid melts into air." *The Communist Manifesto.* Marshall Berman, "the bourgeoisie has a vested interest in destruction." But one day it will go too far. Marx and the Wobblies, giving birth to the new society in the womb of the old. Dreams of the classless society. Tomb and womb. Space of death. Indians with the ghost dance. Starting up again. "Fellow slave" is how the Wobblies addressed each other. Fellow slave. A sign on the pavement:

---

**Nobody is more**
**hopelessly**
**enslaved**
**than those who**
**believe they are free**

---

I look in heaps of garbage for plastic bags to cover us if we try to get some sleep. Huge white plastic bags outside Starbucks look usable. Homeless woman asleep in a doorway, wrapped in an enormous black plastic bag. Right idea. Slight drizzle. Warm. Get to the park. A crazy-looking guy walks by with a sign:

---

**We are the future**
**We are going to win**

---

He is dragging a white dog. He is ready to fight, but his forked fingers mean peace. Some people are ripping open plastic bags. The "human microphone," which everyone spells as "mic check" but is pronounced "mike check," is in full swing, explaining civil disobedience and what to do when arrested. I hook up with my students and with Saa. Magic markers are passed around, for writing the telephone number of the Lawyers' Guild on one's skin. Rain is getting heavier. We are being encouraged to clean the park, which seems absurd to me, because that validates the mayor's excuse for dealing with protesters, as vermin that need extermination . . . time and again, the unclean, the disorderly, the un-uniformed, the un-uniform. And let's not forget the worst, the anarchists, as much vilified by the police as by Marx and Engels.

## We all know
## where the real dirt is

"It has to be cleaned up," the "chief executive" (note the nomenclature) of the management company overseeing the park is reported as saying. The billionaire mayor's girlfriend is on the board of the company that owns the park, and the mayor (according to the *New York Times*, October 15, 2011) "is a mayor obsessed with the cleanliness of the city's public spaces." Later we hear that the management company is way behind in paying its taxes to the city. There are brooms and soap galore, and here I am with a broom, side by side with a merry fellow in a Santa Claus outfit leading the crew. A woman starts up a mic check:

Hello
Hello

I am the sanitation group
I am the sanitation group
(Her voice is shrill, authoritative, nagging)
I am not *the* leader
I am not *the* leader
(long pause)
I am *a* leader
I am *a* leader

The park slopes downhill to the west. Rivers of soapsuds float west merrily along with Santa. Saa loves to clean, and is doing a great job. It feels good to be doing something physical. There are many brooms, all new. No shortage of stuff in Zuccotti Park. This place is organized! Check out the People's Library, the kitchen, the Poets' Corner, the drummers, and the altar. But no time for that now. We are in lockdown, as if a hurricane is imminent. The three thousand or more library books are lovingly bundled into plastic boxes. Together with the poets, the books are the "crown jewels" of this liberated zone, this experiment in "horizontal" decision-making and vertiginous imagination. When the occupation is finally and spectacularly smashed a month later, during the night of November 15th, with riot police beating up protesters and journalists alike, and the night sky humming with police helicopters, the books are thrown into garbage cans and taken away, supposedly to the sanitation garage on 57th Street. Can you imagine! *Sanitation* for books! (And why can't they say *garbage* in this country?) Not to worry.

"Every morning before GA [the general assembly], we would gather on the street and start up the drums," says Danny. "Our efforts channeled the pulse of the occupation." On the first night of occupation he felt drawn to the group of people drumming, singing, and dancing. He had never thought of himself as a musician or a performer, but he felt compelled to pick up a small drum. "As we share this warm harmony," he later wrote, "I decide to burn some incense. It seems others had something similar in mind and soon we are enveloped in candles, smoke, and warmth. While many of us play, a few souls decide to stand up and channel the rhythms into song and rhyme. Out of nowhere these wonderful lyrics emerge full of love, dreams, and longing for the moment of revolution. The space upon which we play is consecrated and transformed."

Next day, the people in the park invented mic check, originally "the people's microphone"—and Danny found himself facilitating the speakers through the process that has come to be called "stacking," whereby your eye is caught by someone in the crowd and you place them on the list. You learn the hand signals quickly down there, and invent just as quickly. Like the mic check, these signals bear the mark of an exotic tribe and secret society, invented yesterday, brushing history against the grain.

It is said that the mic check was invented because of the city ban on microphones in Zuccotti Park. That ban triggered the most powerful invention of the Occupy movement.

Seven months later in Union Square, at the New York May Day march, I saw many of the people who had been in Zuccotti Park, but this time there was something wrong. Instead of the magic of the mic check, there was a powerful public address system dominated by one or two people screaming slogans. There was little chance for the rest of us to converse with each other. The casual atmosphere was gone, as was the chance to hear opposing points of view enjoined by the crowd repeating the speaker as with the mic check. In that situation you rarely felt you were being screamed at or lectured. The easiest way to kill the Occupy movement would be with a centralized public address system, as opposed to the rippling network of wildlife that was Zuccotti.

The weather was unusually balmy in Zuccotti Park in September and October. To visit the park was like going to a street fair.

Photograph by Nancy Goldring.

Photograph by Nancy Goldring.

Photograph by Nancy Goldring.

Photograph by Nancy Goldring.

Photograph by Nancy
Goldring.

There were so many smiling, radiant people, mixed with a few grim, concentrated ones. Some women were topless. Many people were on their hands and knees making signs on brown cardboard recycled from boxes. T-shirts were being silkscreened. As the days went by, older people got into the mix. On the pavement by the park, tourist photographers stood three deep, many engaged in polite but strenuous political, philosophical, and theological debate.

---

### Mutual responsibility
### Come chat with us

---

The park was ablaze with flags: rainbows, the planet earth, and of course Old Glory with the logos of corporations instead of stars. Poor stars, trumped like this. But the trees still had their leaves, fluttering.

Most of all, I was struck by the statuesque quality of many of the people holding up their handmade signs: like centaurs, half-person, half-sign. Looking now at the photographs, which give me some distance from the hurly-burly of the face-to-face realities, I see the sign as an extension of the human figure, that history is being made by this stiller-than-still conjunction, heavy with the weight of ages and the exhilaration of bucking the system. And then I realize that this centaur-like quality and stiller than stillness—this terrible gravitas—occurs because the sign holder is posing

Photograph by author.

Photograph by Nancy Goldring.

for photographers, or rather, because the sign is being made to pose for the camera with its very stillness calling to mind—for the aficionados, at least—that wonderful line of Adorno's in which he tells us that the trick to Benjamin's style is the need to become a thing in order to break the magic spell of things. Compare the statuesque quality of the centaurs with the radiance of the sign come alive.

It is the handmadeness of the signs, their artisanal crudity, art before the age of mechanical or digital reproduction, that facilitates this hop, skip,

Photograph by Nancy Goldring.

and jump. To Nancy Goldring, who took many of the photographs accompanying this essay, it seems as if this graven quality comes from the sign saying exactly what the sign bearer wants to say. Put another way, the sign has a talismanic function, an incantatory drive, and is of divine inspiration, the gods in this case being of mirthful disposition, feeling quite at home in the park.

For a century now, advertising signs and images have stolen from the avant-garde. Now it's payback.

Photograph by Nancy Goldring.

And here we are on the night of October 13th, when the city is going to bring in its sanitation workers, backed by police. The tents have come down.

The park has become a sea of blue tarpaulins glistening with rain, a sea of hope. Is this the sea that Mao talked about in his writings on guerrilla warfare? Are we the waves to which Nietzsche passionately refers in his "Will and Wave," that mighty turbulence breaking on the rocks of time, dashing pearls, holding court with history through secret affinities?

Photograph by the author.

---

**That is how the waves live—that is how we live,
we who will—I will say no more**

---

Zuccotti Park is all that, bathed in an unearthly yellow-green light coming from the streets around. Underneath, hard granite. And underneath that? The beach!

---

**Truly, at this moment nothing remains of the world but
green dusk and green thunderbolts**

---

Like dancers we swirl, floating on high spirits and the sense, no matter how silly, that at least we are accomplishing something by cleaning. Some socks float by. There is a smell of sage burning. Shamans circle the perimeter of the park providing the real cleansing. Scrub away. How absurd!

We use our magic to thwart their magic. They have pepper spray. We have burning sage. They prohibit microphones. We have the people's microphone. They prohibit tents. We improvise tents that are not tents but what nomads used before North Face. They build buildings higher than Egyptian pyramids, but that allows our drumming to reverberate all the louder and our projections of images and e-mails at night to be all the more

Photograph by the author.

Photograph by the author.

visible and magical, taking advantage of the megascreens that the facades of these giant buildings provide.

Each day, each week sees another deterritorialization of their reterritorializatons. They prohibit the electric generators we use for our computers and cell phones. We set up bicycles that can generate power, and people who would otherwise gawk and take photographs get into the movement; they become Dionysian and not just Apollonian, sitting in the saddle and pedaling like crazy. This is how they get into the movement. One woman sees it in historical terms, running in matrilines. As she pedals, smiling, she says, "I can tell my grandchildren I provided energy for Occupy Wall Street."

By her side, several older women sit sedate in lounge chairs knitting woolies for OWS and the coming winter. They have all the time in the world, for they inhabit time and time stands still. They don't need to reference history or the matriline. They are all that with what Benjamin called "the time of the now," that compressed stasis which is the revolutionary moment. Clickety-clack go the knitting needles as history is rewoven. They have cardboard signs by their sides, voicing their outrage. Clickety-clack. This is not the clickety-clack of the locomotive of history which Marx invokes in his preface to *The Introduction to The Critique of Political Economy*. This is not the clickety-clack of Benjamin in his anarchist (Blanqui) mode, trying to figure out when to pull the emergency brake that will usher in the revolution. Nor is it the explosion that Benjamin invokes as the blasting apart of the continuum of history that creates the *jetztzeit*, the "time filled with the presence of the now." Revolution is different now.

Another vision of revolution surfaces: a cheeky little 4×3" sticker adorn-

Photograph by the author.

Photograph by the author.

ing the seventy-foot-high orange metal *Joie de Vivre* sculpture at the southeast corner of the park:

---

**Lick**

**my**

**Goldman**

**Sachs!**

---

Jack the giant-killer! This little fellow transforms the sculpture, another of New York's notable contributions to public art, but that is nothing compared with what has been going on in the park since OWS, where art acquires new meaning as we read here:

---

**This**

**revolution for**

**display**

**purposes**

**only**

---

In the corner of the diminutive sticker, we read:

---

**My money's no whore.   99%**

---

On all sides jackhammers, police sirens, and traffic roaring down Broadway echoes bouncing off buildings. Mic check and the poets keep at it, along with the drums. Mic check: I still can't get over this crazy spelling, a code for the initiated. An assault on the signifier. My own name sometimes gets spelled thus: Mic. So what? Mick check? What is being checked here, anyway? A mic check is a check to ensure that an electronic sound system is functioning, or rather that the channel is open to all sounds. Everyone can have a shot. If anything is emblematic of the movement, this is it. Inadvertently, what we can call "the system," the nervously nervous nervous system (which is also the blue tarpaulin sea), spun Hegel off his feet and gave the dialectic of history another twist, converting the state prohibition of electronic microphones in the park into a magical weapon that is now being copied across the country, if not the world, as a new form of social speech, a new form of being. Michelle tells me that even the police tried to use it once—at the end of the #3 subway line at New Lots, where OWS occupied a foreclosed home. Everyone laughs.

---

**I think they got it wrong. We've been occupied
for years. This occupation is de-occupation.**

---

And why magic? Because of the repetition? In repetition you come to grips with trauma, as will be recognized by some readers of Freud's *Beyond the Pleasure Principle*, a text that in Zuccotti, with "mic check," becomes a living, performed, text, better called *Beyond "Beyond the Pleasure Principle,"* since here death and pleasure (as analyzed in Freud's text) commingle in the exploration of the creative effect of shock in modernity, there being different types of shock at work in OWS.

The shock of the economic system imploding (call it depression/ recession) is one of these shocks. The shock of mounting a challenge (OWS) is quite another, and both types of shock galvanize body and imagination. Shock, it seems to me, speeds things up, but can also slow time down to dead crawl. This is the essence of Zuccotti as people invent new ways of inhabiting time alongside new ways of talking to one another. This is also what makes for the "trance" Danny talked about, a sort of dream-space out of ordinary life and consciousness, yet it also an "awakening," conceptualized by Benjamin as his trope for revolution.[3]

"Beyond the Pleasure Principle" is an essay that starts with shock and ends with the psyche become inorganic matter. Written late in life, this text is famous for Freud's postulate of the death drive since the pleasure principle could not account for much that is basic to human ways. In this larger vision, human history becomes a branch of natural history, the psyche becomes biology—yet it is a strange biology, more like a mystical or metaphysical biology in which "natural history" carries its own cosmic charge, as when the tides turn with the ascent of the moon and the sorcerer's spell gains momentum with song and Nietzsche's "eternal return" enters another spin cycle. Here then is the driving storm tonight, this night, the clashing of elements—thunderous rain and tides of police—as the mayor prepares his NYPD! For what is the death drive but a marvelous giving up, a succumbing—all that negativity which our culture tells us is wrongheaded and unhelpful—yet it is surely part of the libidinal energy that goes into this rebellion against money (see Norman O. Brown, *Life against Death*)? This is the physicality of the natural history at work in Zuccotti Park, the secret of what Solomeyer calls "erotic materialism."

And why magic? Because with mic check, the rhetorical style alters toward the fundamental, the pithy, and the word *jab*. These are shocks too. These are drumbeats of words like the drums that keep going at the west side of the park, where what people call "the right brain" functions in contrast and as complementary to "the left brain" on the east side of the park (the higher side, of course), where mic checkers get their chance, and where the "general assemblies" take place every day.

And why magic? Because there is a religious wave, an African and/or African-American thing going on here, with the repetition of the pastor's words by the listeners. We hear together. We repeat together. And in that repetition we first hear, then speak, thereby tasting the words in our mouths like cherries, with time to let the ideas settle. The idea part of the spoken word gets its chance to resonate in different dimensions of thought and of feeling.

There can be fear here, too: fear of mindless repetition of the brain-

---

3. See Convolute K, "Dream City and Dream House, Dreams of the Future, Anthropological Nihilism, Jung," in *The Arcades Project*, by Walter Benjamin, ed. Rolf Tiedemann, trans. Howard Eiland and Kevin McLaughlin (Cambridge, MA: Belknap Press of Harvard University Press, 1999), 388.

washed. This is the cultic expression of magic. But then the next mic checker gets up, and the message is quite different from the last one! We repeat, yet we transform. And think of Allen Ginsberg with his harmonium and his *OOM, OOM*, and many more *OOMs*. There is joy in spoofing the too-serious ones, left-wing or right-wing, as well as the academic experts—plenty of them—who come here to illuminate the dark spaces. Remember Debs, the ultimate seduction? "I will not lead you into the Promised Land because if I do, others can lead you out."

This is worth thinking about. Occupying Wall Street inevitably means occupying how we talk in public, how we learn and teach, and how we write ethnography (about our own tribe). All this is up for grabs. Otherwise there is no occupation.

The occupation is self-reflexive to a fault.

True. But we are also the nervy nervous ones awaiting attack. In the wan, green light our sea ripples over the shoals of the nervous system. We are awaiting the police, who at the moment form around two sides of the park. On the north side their blue-and-white cars and vans face us, ready to leap. Behind the cars stands a skyscraper crisscrossed by dark steel beams, like a fortress. An art student from Parsons tells me it is the FBI building. In bold black letters on the facade, as I recall:

---

**One Liberty Plaza**

---

By 2 a.m. it is pouring. There is lightning and thunder. The heavens erupt. Reality mimics art, by which I mean John Cage's 1976 performance *Lecture on the Weather*, in which art mimics reality, the reality of a storm. Cage devised this performance for the Canadian Broadcasting Corporation, to mark the US bicentenary. Twelve speakers recite at the same time different passages selected by chance from Thoreau's *Civil Disobedience* until, about half an hour later, with a swelling hubbub of voices on the stage, lightning flashes and thunderclaps bring history (civil disobedience) and natural history (the storm) together.

The crowd has thinned. The commercial food stands on the south side of the park are doing a great business. Their warmth, light, and sense of bounty are cheering. I meet up with students from Columbia. We mix and mingle, talking, smoking, animated, searching for shelter, waiting for the bust, scenarios of the impending attack running through our minds. Many people prefer to stand, shifting from one foot to another, finding friends, meeting strangers, forming a strange new community of the righteous and the beleaguered. Classic concepts leap to mind—especially the "liminal space" Victor Turner illuminated for us from his studies in southern Africa in the 1950s, where the initiates were gathered and transformed step by step through rituals and symbols resonant with myth. Being betwixt and between, the initiates occupy a magical space in which the elementary forms of religious life take fire. The twin poles of birth and death frame the space. Womb and tomb.

"I asked my friend why he always wears that scarf," says Danny. "He's wearing the scarf that he wore on the first night of the occupation. I ask him why he always carries that scarf around him wherever he goes. He tells me it's like his baby blanket. 'On September 17 I died. On September 17 I began living. I found this scarf that day. It is a relic from the rebirth, from the moment when I started taking my first steps in this new life, in this new me.'"

Tomb and womb. A child is born from the womb just as spirits emerge from the tomb. *Emergence* is the trope. Emergence from the underworld. Orpheus, don't look back! Not this time! Sing your songs so beautiful they enchant animals and things such as these buildings reaching the sky, this Wall Street so mythical and world-dominating. "Mr. Gorbachev, tear down this wall," said the Great Communicator.

But what have we here? Weeks later, I see a photograph of a tall young man with camouflage pants, a black cowboy hat, and a big smile. He is standing on the perimeter of Zuccotti Park along Broadway with a young girl on his shoulders who is holding up a sign. Her mouth is wide open. Is it surprise? Is she challenging us? As always, the faces of the people holding the signs say as much as the signs themselves, and the signs say plenty. What is she holding up?

---

**Mr. Obama
tear down
this wall**

---

Looking for a new language? Well, here it is: the language of the sign, the language of wit rearranging history through a barrage of A-*Effekts* that warp what we have taken for real. It is a scene-language, like that on Brecht's placards hung above the stage. "Mr. Obama, tear down this wall!"

## I'm so angry that
## I made a sign

There is no doubt a morality play is taking place here, powered by the "moral economy" that the historian E. P. Thompson brought to our attention. This is bigger than terms like "growing income disparity" or "We are the 99 percent" convey—terms encumbered by the economism they challenge. "The rupture between bodies and homes, the rupture of foreclosure," writes Michelle, whose own family was foreclosed in Los Angeles, "is revelatory—spirits of home emerge as well as the specters of power. The taking of a home by a bank is experienced as a violation of sacred space." Thompson analyzed eighteenth-century bread riots in London. Today it's homes.

The Global City we hear so much about gets its comeuppance. There was the rancor of 9/11 as the margins of empire struck back a few blocks from here. Ten years later, there was Tahrir Square, downtown Cairo, then Gezi Park in Istanbul, yesterday Hong Kong.

Peter Lamborn Wilson put his pen and paints to work to make a poster which on April 20, 2011, he mailed from Cairo, a lamentably poor town in upstate New York. He mailed copies to the Gallery of the Surrealist Movement in Cairo, to the Egyptian National Museum, and to Egyptians in the United States, asking them to send it on to friends in Cairo. He also mailed a few to people like me.

**Wake up America**
**Be like Egypt**
**Fatimid Order of Cairo, NY, greets Cairo, Egypt, Tahrir Square**
**Overthrow all pharaohs**
**Power to the world of the imagination**
**Be-sphinxed**

Monstrous masks and transgression are de rigueur in the liminal period. In OWS this is manifest in outrage transformed automatically into humor and play, and likewise by the NYPD into its growl, pepper spray, and medieval riot gear. The atomized mass of yesterday, without hope, has crystallized into a community defining itself through a new language and sense of collective. It is a movement that seems to have come out of nowhere, a messianic movement after the death of God that kindles our polymorphously perverse infancy with relish. More than anything else it is an attitude, a mood, an atmosphere, like John Cage's babbly lecture on weather mixing up Thoreau's *Civil Disobedience* with thunder and lightning, and this is why the politicians and the experts have a problem. They see OWS as primitive and diffuse because it has no precise demands—as if the demand for equality were not a demand, at once moral and economic, redefining personhood and reality itself. OWS is akin to the "primitive rebels" that Eric Hobsbawm called the 1920s and 30s anarchists of Spain, a movement he saw as "pre-political." What the experts want is for OWS to submit to the language of the prevailing system. Yet is it not the case that merely to articulate such is to sell out the movement? There is as yet no language to express the "drift," as Lyotard called it, with '68 in mind. Politics as aesthetics is back. Politics as "affective intensity" is back too. "A successful attack on the belief in necessity would inevitably lead to the destruction of kapital's very main- spring," he wrote back then. The laws of equivalence are in suspense, and libidinal impulses are unhooked from prevailing norms. But the experts want to channel the messianic and transgressive impulse into their own need for pathological fame and power.

Saa finds a granite step that can serve as a backrest for sleeping while sitting. The plastic keeps off some of the rain, but everything is wet now. We doze, flitting between sleep and waking, bathed in that eerie green-

Photograph by the author.

yellow light that makes the sea of tarpaulins glisten, while beneath are bodies forming waves and hillocks, like seals on the beach, vague outlines of animated beings pushing through. Is that our movement? Is that OWS, with its eerie green-yellow light and glistening tarp surfaces, with animal-like shapes pushing through? On the south side of the park where we lie, the rain beats down with demonic fury, and a crude sign in large white letters stands out above the police barriers: "Liberty and justice for all."

5:50 a.m.: sudden mic check. "Breaking news" (funny how they reproduce the media, especially at this crucial moment). The park has filled to overflowing in the past dark hour, along with rising tension, and three "echoes" or rebootings of the mic check are required to get to the people at the back.

> Breaking news
> Breaking news
> Breaking news

The human microphone is bursting to capacity. Echoes chase echoes, and only the most alert ears and powerful voices are able to transmit anything. Hope and fear blur the message. The faces in the sea of faces around me in the magic hour of dawn are faces of angels and trust. We bond. We embrace with our eyes. You strain forward, then pivot 180 degrees to catch the repetition. We feel the incredible power of repetition—each repetition the same, each one slightly off. ("What did they say?") It could be natural forces: that sea, those waves again, that muffled thunder, on our side, now, natural force, natural history.

---

**The deputy mayor
has canceled the cleanup.**

---

For a second a stunned silence
Then cheers of unbelievable elation
A young man asks for a mic check

---

**Look up
Look up
Look up**

**See the sky**
**See the sky**
**See the sky**

**A new dawn**
**A new dawn**
**A new dawn**

---

Mist clings to the skyscrapers. The mottled sky grows pink with promise of light. My sun, 'tis of thee. For a glorious moment, history and natural history fuse. Second nature dissolves. The time of the now.

---

**Clickety clack**
**Clickety clack**
**Clickety clack**

---

Photograph by the author.

# Two Weeks in Palestine
*My First Visit*

**Thursday June 17, 2013:** I pretty well stopped eating in Palestine, not because I wasn't offered food at every turn, but because the intensity ate me alive. It was like I was breathing different air on a different planet where the customary laws of gravity and physics no longer existed. Except it wasn't just the harsh reality of physics—of land occupation and checkpoints and the permits required for any and everything—but the even harsher reality of things harder for me to pin down. Paranoia? Yes. Anxiety? Yes. But these terms are too obvious yet not quite right, anyway. Above all what threw me was the patience and calm in the midst of choppy seas that in an instant could become a gale inside and outside. Was it that things seemed calm, but shouldn't? Or was it that people spent a lot of time making calm, if you see what I mean, and that this was a sort of national pastime, a gargantuan cultural feat, "making calmness." (Compare with the agitated frenzy I always hear about in Israel.) Or is it that no matter how bad a situation, people adapt and life continues in its steady and unsteady rhythms, as it must for the forty-year-old man I met in the subterranean market in Hebron selling spices at the same stall all his life and who has never seen the sea, holding my arm, eyes burning, when I tell him I am from Sydney. Although it is quite close, he has never seen the sea

I was accompanied by the Helsinki-based artist, Carolina Trigo, the first week in Ramallah and Hebron, and later by Vivien Sansour who lives in the West Bank and writes on the lives of Palestinian farmers. I owe much to Lara Khaldi of the Sakakini Cultural Center, to Shuruq Harb, Sameer Khriesh, and especially to Rania Jawad and Ala Azeeh, all of Ramallah as well as to Ati Citron of Tel Aviv. Filmmaker Hadeel Assali set the wheels in motion. For their comments on an earlier version of this diary I am much indebted to Hadeel Assali, Lauren Berlant, Amahl Bishara, Christina Carter, Amy Franceschini, Thavolia Glymph, Nancy Goldring, Lisa Hajjar, Roger Heacock, Tom Mitchell, Eleni Myrivilli, Stephen Muecke, Vivien Sansour, Daphne Skillen, and Roelof Smilde.

because he doesn't have a permit to travel the necessary roads. But the spices need to be gathered from the dusty hillsides, the customers expect it, and he has to live, sea-less as it may be. Twenty meters away Jewish settlers are said to pour garbage and even urine down into the marketplace from their houses which not so long ago were the homes of Palestinians whom, by and large, Israelis insist on calling "Arabs" as if the very word *Palestine* does not exist, is not allowed to exist, and yet for all of that non-existence very much exists—as a taboo word threatening thought itself and, indeed, the very writing of this diary. Never have I felt the use of names and words to be so precarious.

**Friday:** In Palestine I was forever struck by the gulf between violence and the manner by which it was related, as with the seller of spices in Hebron or a young man in Ramallah relating his arrest at the age of seventeen by Israeli soldiers at his home early one morning. No lights. No sirens. A stone thrown through the window shattering the glass at two in the morning. Opening the door into that black night what seemed like hundreds of Israeli soldiers aiming red laser beams on his chest through the scopes of their guns. A hooded informer pushed forth to identify him. Blindfolded, hands and ankles cuffed, beaten and tortured three days, trussed to a chair with a strong light in front of his face. When he nodded off, a surveillance camera caught him and he was once again woken up for questioning. Ten to a cell, one toilet which doubled up as a "shower," and. thirteen hours a day studying. He learned Hebrew by reading the newspaper his uncle sent him each day.

You've seen it all in the movies, I'm sure. Many times.

But not this, not the way he told it, sitting cross legged in the soft grass of the Khalil Sakakini cultural center in Ramallah mid-afternoon beneath a dark fig tree. As he spoke, picking up a blade of grass now and again, two kittens played as I peeled unripe figs on the ground. Free of pain or malice, his voice was like a slow-moving river occasionally dislodging a stone on the riverbed, the voice of the saints.

Living in the West Bank, I came to understand, is like living under that same sleep-depriving light. The entire population inhabits this prison, being allowed a little exercise each day, so long as the prison guards allow it, and this is made worse, or at least extra frustrating, I am continuously assured, since the Oslo peace accords of 1993, because now the Palestinian Authority undertakes much of the Israeli policing in the name of the Palestinians themselves.

But then I recall a different pattern of tension and calm, or apparent calm, in the insistent, brooding, face of Mohammed, shrouded in smoke and darkness, always out on the little terrace of the apartment, his lookout post, where he sat chain smoking and reading hour after hour. A donkey brayed—*hee hah, hee hah*, piercing the hot air like it was vomiting its heart out, ours included. *Hee hah, hee hah*, reverberating in the sun-baked hills while in the distance on the ridge was a military outpost surrounded by settlers. The heat bore down. Time stopped. No matter how many questions I asked—because everything he explained begged more questions—he patiently answered in a carefully articulated manner which, for all its lawyer-like cadence and logic, endeared me to him, each link in the chain drawing out the next like a magician bringing colored ribbons without end from his mouth. His entire body was in that speech, taking me out of my own.

Could this articulation of bodies through stories that lead to other stories be evidence of the wearing away of spirit that people say is the basic strategy of Occupation? Hardly. For this is a nation of storytellers with no end in sight, well aware that "not even the dead shall be safe."

But what then of me and my stories?

These are stories licensed by that disconcerting halo of innocence granted the guest, visitor to an unknown land with his stumbling gait of perception. And because of the newness, of it all, of his ignorance, of it all, and the other worldliness, of it all, like James Agee long ago in Alabama, such a person may now and again find him or herself, if the stars be right, in that zen position where blindness and insight converge, or at least, overlap. Famously Agee referred to this as "the effort to perceive simply the cruel radiance of what is."

How can I, the stranger, who teaches in the US and does not live this situation, find that crooked path avoiding its exoticization while trying to crack the stupendous indifference to it? For it is exotic, this brazen and sadistic cruelty exercised routinely by the Occupiers, meaning in the first instance the settlers and the soldiers, just as people outside of Palestine seem indifferent to it. Surely institutionalized cruelty has existed since the world began, but what happens in Palestine is dependent on the manipulated indifference of the US taxpayers underwriting Israel and on strategically funded mouthpieces of public opinion according to which support of Palestine is treason or something close to it and support for Israel has become a patriotic, if not holy, obligation. Nobody who has said anything critical of Israel or is supportive of the Palestinians is going to have an easy time getting appointed to a US government or even a university post nowadays, all of which evokes memories of earlier moral crusades in the US, let alone the exclusion of Jews from universities and other worthy institutions such as golf clubs.

And if that's not enough, we must not be so naive as to think that the visitor, like myself, however shocked and filled with rage, is not also fascinated by this horror and, to that extent, in a complex way, complicit with it. This alone makes such storytelling and retelling a treacherous activity. Joseph Conrad called it "the fascination of the abomination," an accurate if ponderous rendering of the stock in trade of war journalists and war photographers, especially the latter, wild men and wild women to the core, too much in love with their work which soon settles into banality. But that is as nothing compared with the conceit of the reader of their work, secure at one remove from the action, yet no less likely to be buoyed up by the tempestuous currents of attraction and repulsion inflaming it before succumbing to indifference and turning the page or clicking the mouse.

Strategically short on explanation as one day follows the next in blind submission not to narrative but to time's roll of the dice, it is my hope that the flexibility and "multi-tasking" to be found in the fieldworker's diary can reconfigure this otherwise paralyzing "fascination of the abomination." Like the magical shield of Perseus, a diary allows of witness without being turned to stone. Like Walter Benjamin's *Denkbilden* or "thought-images," the diary form facilitates grasping those images that flare up at a moment of danger when the potential for innervating the body is at its highest.

I fear I am not expressing this well enough. In Palestine I was flooded with stories, each one precipitating the next in an endless flow, each one shocking, yet everyday. It was not that people made light of their circumstance or resisted horror with humor. No. More to the point was that people were capable, precisely because of their circumstance, of combining the unthinkable with the sayable—*that* was the miracle—and hence pass the baton of witnessing along to me, to pass on to you in the hope, vain as it may be, that witnessing becomes something more than consumption. Like travel and anthropology, reading has not only its passions but responsibilities, too.

**Saturday:** Driving back to Ramallah early evening Sameer mentioned that the song used for a man asking for the hand of a woman is also sung collectively by people greeting the corpse of a person killed by Israeli soldiers. It stopped me in my tracks. He was pretty well chain smoking as he drove with a beer in the other hand, guiding the car through whiplash curves up and down the stony hillsides most of which have Israeli settlements on the ridge as part of the now "natural" landscape guarding the expansion each day deeper into what is left of Palestine.

He was referring to what is called Zaghareet, that spine-chilling sound we call *ululation*, pitching reality into a wholly different register of being that Georges Bataille, for one, would have no hesitation calling "sacred." Later a friend explains that mothers are encouraged to sing when they find out their son or daughter has been killed by the Israeli soldiers. It is a way of expressing in almost religious terms that he has not died in vain. Unlike weddings with their songs relaying happy occasions and love, the women are sobbing—"a contradiction so excessive so tremendous and so hard to watch, a prime example of the paradoxes and the crazy making you describe in your writing."

After we dropped his mother off in Ramallah, where she gave me a bouquet of the sweetest-smelling jasmine she told me to put under my pillow, a fragrance that drove us wild in the confines of the car, Sameer drove to the end of the street. Before us pitch black was a valley with a solitary light weaving its way slowly through it. That was Palestinian land, he said. Now it's militarized and that, pointing to a nub of darkness down below in the blackness, is a prison with about seven hundred political prisoners, forty of whom are on hunger strike. On top of the dark valley lights blazed. Look! That's Jerusalem, where I cannot go. Only look!

We sat for what seemed an eternity looking at Jerusalem winking at us in the hot night as he lit another cigarette.

Right now, he said, there are some 1,400 political prisoners in the West Bank (which seemed to me a small number—and I was later told it was unusually small), but as I listened to Palestinians I felt prison was the least important part of the Israeli choke hold because the whole of the West Bank is a prison and I guess Gaza more so.[1]

---

1. As of late July 2013, the more exact figure is 5,059, including a five-year-old taken into custody by the IDF. The Palestinian population of the West Bank and Gaza is around four million. A friend comments:

> Most or all of the prisoners are not held in the West Bank, but in Israel and prisoners are a really hot issue now, with talk of a release of the prisoners who were arrested before Oslo (1993). You mention below about political dates punctuating lives here. In my circles, the numbers about prisoners do too—my brother in law is one of the 104 prisoners who is supposed to be released during this new round of negotiations; we've been talking for days and days about the 26 prisoners who should be released in the first installment, and about how my brother in law was on a list published in an Israeli paper (and republished widely). But no one ever

It is a bewildering thing to be a prisoner in your own land. Imagine nobody resident in Brooklyn is allowed to go to Times Square unless they have a special permit, something very few people can ever get. Imagine you cannot use La Guardia, Kennedy, or Newark airports, but have to somehow finagle your way with a myriad of permits and IDs to Canada (by which I mean the airport in Amman, Jordan, crossing the Allenby Bridge—note the name) in order to board a plane. And, of course, many cannot even do that.

Imagine a straight line access between the cities of this tiny land. Then imagine a tortuous, snakelike twisting labyrinth of narrow and sometimes dangerous roads criss-crossing these immaculate straight roads reserved for settlers racing from their hilltop redoubts to work or pick up their US taxpayer funded welfare checks in Tel Aviv or Jerusalem half an hour away while you wait at checkpoints sometimes for hours, hoping it isn't closed that day and that fate will be kind to you and let you through. If traveling by bus you disembark, then walk through narrow chutes behind the person in front—like cattle—pause for an arbitrary length of time before the turnstile clicks open thanks to an invisible or barely visible soldier in a sentry box gazing through a slit or at a computer screen. You show your papers then shuffle into another chute, and maybe a third one. And, of course, some people never make it through. Imagine you are an adult living in Ramallah only a few miles from Jerusalem or the Mediterranean but have never once been able to visit Jerusalem or seen the sea.

Finally, if you are still able to imagine anything, imagine that all the names of areas, towns, and hamlets are changed into the language of the occupier and this is done not by choosing some wildly different name but one that is close, in pronunciation, to the occupier's language which is then transcribed back into the written language of the occupied in a dizzying process of appropriation, expropriation, and extermination.

An example I find in a book discusses a sign by the roadway for the Jordan Valley. The Hebrew name of the valley is on top in Hebrew. The name "Jordan Valley" in English is in the middle. And the name *Wadi Yardin* is on

---

said that list was organized by when the prisoners would be released—it was organized in terms of date of arrest. . . . But what else is there to think about, aside from these numbers? Other numbers: he has been in prison for 22 years, and my mother-in-law's friend's son has been in for 29 years, and the longest serving political prisoner of the group has been behind bars for 30 years. As we wait to hear about my brother-in-law, the family has installed new lighting in the house they built for him, repainted the walls in fashionable textured beige paint, put in granite countertops in the kitchen.

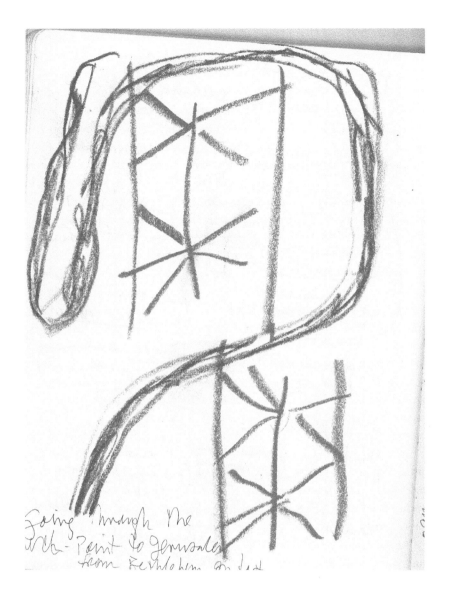

Going through the
Wall - Point to Jerusalem
from Bethlehem on left

the bottom, in Arabic. But the Arabic name for the valley is actually *Wadi al-Urdon*. What the sign does is to transliterate the Hebrew name, *Yardin*, in Arabic letters.[2]

A correction. Is it extermination? Is it the obliteration of the named landscape of memory essential to community and tradition? Or is it rather

2. Nasser Abufarha, *The Making of a Human Bomb: An Ethnology of Palestinian Resistance* (Durham, NC: Duke University Press, 2009), 114–15.

that in choosing a word that is close in pronunciation but not the same, what results is the humiliating reminder of domination and submission? If someone forces me to change one letter in the pronunciation and writing of my name so that, for instance I become Mike instead of Mick, am I and my friends and family not constantly reminded of the once was and of the change forced every time the tongue sets to work altering what is, in effect, a universe of meaning?

But then, I wonder if Palestinians actually do use these new names, anyway? In which case, of what use are they? They seem more like flags of the state of Israel stuck awkwardly in Palestinian soil or like the equally awkward settlements always located on hilltops, like fortresses, even though they can also pass for some sort of dream kitsch American suburb, while the homes of the Palestinian peasants hug the contours of the valleys below.

**Sunday:** In a camp in Bethlehem I sat drinking coffee with a young photographer, Mohammad Al-Azza, who directs the media unit of a nearby youth center. A huge black key lies above a keyhole shaped gateway to the camp, the key being the great symbol of Return, the key to the house and home from which we were forced by the occupiers who now live in our home—our country—as if it were theirs. On a nearby wall was a portrait of a smiling Leila Khaled, the great hijacker of commercial aircraft in the 1970s.

Earlier I was shown some of his photographs that chronicle the life of the camp founded in the wake of the 1948 war. We sat in the shade of the patio of his extended family's three-story stone and concrete home from where I was acutely conscious of the infamous wall that separates Israel from the Occupied Territory and Palestinian communities from each other. Barely two hundred meters away, there was a sniper's tower built into and rising above the wall, visible if you tilted your head to one side of an old palm tree peeling great husks of brown bark into the patio.

Six years ago, he told me, with the aid of a translator, his thirteen-year-old cousin was shot through the abdomen by a sniper from that tower while playing on the balcony of the third story.[3] Why? Why indeed. And now his brother is facing the possibility of five years in prison. Mohammad was himself shot badly on April 8th this year, a bare two months back, by the IDF trying, I am told, to stop his photography and teaching.[4] He spent

3. Most of the people I met spoke English which seems widespread in the West Bank.
4. See the article by Ahmal Bishara on his shooting in April: http://photography.jadaliyya.com/pages/index/11245/a-camera%E2%80%99s-view-finder-confronts-a-gun-sight.

weeks in the hospital and needs more surgery on his face. I was unaware of this until three days later for he sat quiet and relaxed, at ease with the world. Or maybe the attack on him was mentioned but in such a casual way and in such a melee of conversations that it passed over me or, more likely and as with so many stories in Palestine, it spent itself in the white heat of its intensity.

Next to the palm tree in the patio there was an old olive tree showering us in the delicate shade of its silver greenery. Can a symbol be so exquisitely symbolic that it is more than a symbol? Along the road into Bethlehem from Ramallah I saw rows of black stumps about thirty centimeters high, the wounded remains of Palestinian olive groves cut down by the Israeli state so as to prevent attacks on the road. At least that was what I was told. But then what cover does an olive grove provide since the trees are generally bare two meters up from the ground and offer no hiding place?

Those blackened stumps, like so many amputated limbs, are more than wounded remains. They seem like gravestones aligned in neat rows and diagonals as the settlers rewrite history beginning with the cultivated landscape itself. In this makeover of history, the olive tree is profoundly implicated, the arche symbol of Palestinian ownership of the land, "ownership" in the organic sense of what Marx, following Aristotle, called "use value."

Later I saw olive trees by the side of the road that had been torched by settlers. Given the oil in the trees, it must be quite a sight for the settlers to see an olive grove ablaze, something biblical, you could say, biblical and prophetic, suggesting the wrath of God smiting the infidel, wreaking destruction on all sides.

Three things told me:

Very few settlers plant or cultivate the olive. They do, however, steal Palestinian olive trees.

"Destroying olive trees means the land is not cultivated, which makes it state-owned according to military laws in the occupied territories."

Since 2007 the olive tree is the national tree of Israel.

What are we to make of this?

*Olive Tree = Nature= Palestinian Old = (what will become) Israeli Old*
*Olive Tree = Archaic Symbol (Jung) = Dialectical Image (Benjamin)*

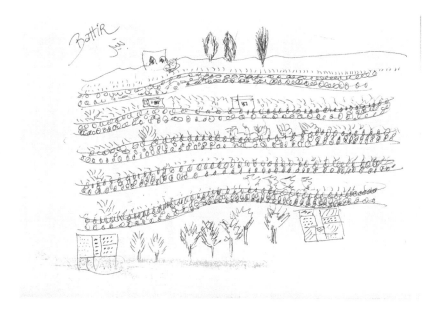

The Israeli state adores trees, does it not? The Israeli state is Green, is it not, "making the desert bloom" and all that, as if what the Zionists encountered was, as they say, "a land without people for a people without land," an uncultivated "desert." Hence the zeal with which the Jewish National Fund has been planting trees since 1948, continuing the work of the British Empire planting fast-growing pines—not native to the region—especially on borders between Israeli settlements and Palestinian farmland so as to conceal the prior existence of Palestinian villages and extend Israeli settlement, so I am told by the peasants of Battir village near Bethlehem. This village boasts a wonderfully efficient irrigation system dating before Roman times. Today eight clans share the water, one clan a day, making an eight day week. How anyone could have thought of this land as a desert is beyond me. Despite the predations of Israeli settlers I see intricate terracing of the hillsides in many places in the West Bank, meticulous and beautiful, existing long before Zionism. [5]

My guide tells me people tried to get these Battir terraces and farmland

---

5. On the Internet I read that in September 2007 the olive was elected the national tree of the state of Israel; also note that the national emblem is a shield which contains a menorah in its center, two olive branches on both sides of the menorah and at the bottom the label "Israel." The emblem was designed by the brothers Gabriel and Maxim Shamir, and was officially chosen on February 10, 1949, from among many other proposals submitted as part of a design competition held in 1948.

UNESCO heritage status but the Palestinian Authority blocked that effort saying that in light of the John Kerry visit "it would be an offense to Israel."

On the Internet site for the Jewish National Fund:

CHILDREN'S FOREST CERTIFICATE

The Children's Forest certificate features a patchwork quilt of children planting trees in Israel. Send this certificate to someone special for a birth or Bar/Bat Mitzvah celebration.

$18 a tree

Soon the terraced and irrigated hillside of Battir will be separated from the hillside opposite by the infamous Israeli security wall twisting its way along the valley floor. Already planted in pines, the hill opposite will become all the more securely Israeli with a new name and identity, "The John F. Kennedy National Park," under the protection of the Israeli environmental protection agency (the KKL).

Ecology; an important weapon of oppression.

Seated on the narrow path leading alongside the stone terracing, an old peasant man tells our guide, Hassan, as the shadows lengthen, that lately there have been attacks by rampaging gazelles and wild boar emerging from that John F. Kennedy National Park, destroying their crops.

Gazelles! I cannot believe my ears. Such beauty, grace, and speed, straight from fairy tales and children's books, rampaging with those rougneck red-eyed boars, spectral beings fast of hoof with the determination of tanks flashing tusks and razor-backed bristle necks, prehistory on the run.

What is more — much more — according to the old peasant it seems that the gazelles and the boars are trained somehow to respond to Israeli commands. The peasants hear strange whistles and other sounds emanating from the pines at the times of attack. Has to be in his imagination, right? Magical realism on the frontier harnessing the forces of nature in the form of mythic animals, newly made pine forests, all framed by the magic of that mythic name; "The John F. Kennedy National Park."

The Battir peasants cannot attack the animals which, they tell me, are protected by Israeli law, this being designated as an "Area C" (meaning completely under Israeli control, as is some 80 percent of the territory of the West Bank), and Palestinians cannot have guns, anyway.

Later in the home of a seventy-year-old peasant by name of Abu Nidal,

several miles away on a different hillside, I heard of Israeli soldiers uprooting his oldest olive trees which are he thinks over a thousand years old. Did I hear right? Over a thousand years old. And this spoken with utter casualness and matter of factness as I heard on several other occasions when face to face with the gnarled and twisted, deeply creased and crevassed trunks of such trees, a meter and half thick, or more. On account of their age he calls them *Rumi*, meaning *Roman*.[6] Some Israelis, he explained, sell such trees on the black market for thousands of dollars to Israelis anxious to have such a *Rumi* in front of their home (a "home" which may well have been what the Israelis call an "Arab" home taken during the war of 1948). It must be quite a feat, I thought to myself, to uproot a tree that size and that age with such care that it can be replanted.

---

6. I discover that the name Rumi was applied in medieval Asia Minor to the lands of what was the Eastern Roman empire. Cemal Kafadar, *Between Two Worlds: The Construction of the Ottoman State* (Berkeley: University of California Press, 1995), 1–2.

What is the idea here? That with your newly purchased olive tree you, too, belong to history, like a tree? But, of course, it has to be more than that. After all the tree is a transplant, becoming more like a war trophy. So what sort of fantasy are you rooting yourself into with your *rumi* olive tree? Is this not a form of Occupation too, not of the West Bank but of your Self?

Shortly before taking his own life in 1940, Walter Benjamin, infamous for blending the Kabbalah with Marx and Proust, wrote that not even the dead are safe from the struggle over the images that have the capacity to open memory in novel ways so that the present might change. These *dialectical images*, as he called them, come and go with electrifying speed and, if possible, have to be grasped before they disappear once again. Such is the olive tree, its actual reality and the reality of its disappearance.

Benjamin took his own life but never took up his friend Scholem's repeated invitation to emigrate to British occupied Palestine in the thirties. Nevertheless his last writing, penned in 1940, on the catastrophe that is history, can now be read as if written for Palestine and Palestinians both then and now.

**Monday:** Regarding the olive tree and attempts against all manner of Israeli obstruction to export "Fair Trade" bottles of organic, Palestinian olive oil (known as Canaan) to Europe and the US, someone told me, "You know, the bottle of olive oil is a great activist."

Centered in Jenin, this export business, is the brainchild of an indefatigable Palestinian businessman, Nasser Abufarha, who has a restaurant in Madison, Wisconsin, which is where he wrote his PhD thesis in anthropology at the University of Wisconsin. Later it became a book published by Duke University Press in 2009 entitled *The Making of a Human Bomb*.

Water is a problem for the Palestinian farmers in the Jenin area and elsewhere because the Israeli state prohibits their tapping into sub-surface water. Only Israeli farmers and settlers can do that. That is why Palestinian farmers make plastic canals running between greenhouses to catch rain water off the roofs which is then channeled into ponds. How long before the Israeli state makes it necessary to have a permit to use the rain (or, for that matter, for the rain to rain)?

After all, is there any nature anymore in Palestine where unstinting military occupation surely aims to control all of nature? Why not claim the rain as state property? The greenhouses, too, they are a novelty, an artificial means for intensifying production in an increasingly capital and chemical based agriculture such that nature qua nature disappears, or exists in complicated fusions with technology. A young man in a rented greenhouse shows me with the precision of a watchmaker how he has become a human bee. Deftly he transfers pollen from male to female plants by hand, a delicate and sensuous sexual act that leaves me slightly disturbed. Never did I think I would see mimesis on this intimate scale. "No bees anymore," this human bee tells me, and he blames their absence on Israeli farmers spraying cotton with insecticides.

Not to worry, however, if you're fed up with manual pollination, because now for a mere hundred dollars you can buy from an Israeli kibbutz a small cardboard box containing a few bumble bees. These little tykes dwarf your ordinary bee and can battle their ways through strong headwinds.

**Tuesday:** In a café in Ramallah I ask a young performance artist whether she has worked with Israeli artists. Is there much collaboration? She winces, then tells me she was recently asked to contribute an essay to a book being put together by Israeli artists and she responded she might, but would prefer to write instead on why she was being asked. Her offer was rejected. Or was it that she never heard back? A poet writes that "that I am very uncomfortable framing the situation as two people who just need to get along and who just don't understand each other. I have found that, unfortunately, the reality of a military occupation becomes clouded when the message of 'bridging gaps of understanding between two people who just don't get along' is perpetuated. It is like having to sit down with my rapist and understand his pain while he is still penetrating me."

**Wednesday:** It seemed we were never quite sure if we were legal when driving in the West Bank. Through some vagrant desire for freedom or genuine bewilderment or simple derring do, she would push the car onto an Israeli settler road and hope for the best. Israelis drive cars with yellow plates, Palestinians white ones, so its pretty obvious if you are in the wrong place. Once at night we hit a traffic jam which looked like there might be a police or army checkpoint up front and she immediately turned the car around and sought out the safe road, meaning the Palestinian road, meaning a longer, curvy, and perhaps dangerous road, especially at night, because of poor upkeep.

Space in the West Bank is divided in three. There is the A area (Palestinian Authority administration and security), the B area (PA admin but

Israeli Defense Force security), and the C area (IDF admin *and* security), by far the largest. But it seemed there was another area we could call "the X area," as well, the "gray area," and that's the one most Palestinians are caught in because the colonial "system" created by the Israeli state keeps evolving overlapping and contradictory rules ensuring uncertainty and arbitrariness as the tools of Occupation because like all systems it has its holes, opacities, and contradictions, what I elsewhere call "the Nervous System" adrift on an asymptotic curve ever closer to self-destruction.

In this regard the peasant I mentioned earlier, Abu Nidal, struck me as one of those almost natural phenomena (another human bee?) that bureaucracy and bullying can neither cope with nor comprehend. I say "natural" because he not only had a story to tell but he was the story—as Benjamin describes in his essay on the storyteller being the embodiment of the tale, like Primo Levi with his tale of survival in Auschwitz which is where many of my relatives perished. The original title in Italian is something like *If This Be Man*, suggesting, to me at least, that all of us are included and none of us innocent or know how we will behave when the chips are down.

Now as the wall approaches, Abu Nidal and his daughter are being forced off this, their second farm, to which, via a refugee camp, they relocated after the village in which they previously lived, on the hillside opposite, was demolished by the Israeli state to make way for a national park of pine trees. Could the pine trees have come from a bumper crop of Children's Forest Certificates which feature "a patchwork quilt of children planting trees in Israel"?

Reduced to roughly a quarter its size, their current farm is surrounded on three sides by an electrified fence built by the Israeli state, the remaining side being the great dividing wall to come. God knows why the Israelis built this electrified fence around their house. (Does there have to be a reason?)

Because one of Abu Nidal's grandparents was Muslim and the other Christian they could not be buried in the same cemetery. Therefore, they were buried together on this farm next to the walnuts, apricots, purple plums, yellow plums, oak trees, and fennel, the only problem being that the grave now exists on the other side of the great dividing wall being built by the Israelis.[7]

---

7. See Vivien Sansour, "Exhuming Hope from the Graves," published by (Tustin, CA: Institute for Middle East Understanding, 2012), http://www.imeu.net http://imeu.net/news/article0023007.shtml.

For the moment a solution—if that's the word—has been found. The state of Israel built a concrete lined underground tunnel under the path of the wall so he and his family can visit and tend the grave, provided of course (1) they have a permit and (2) tolerate a surveillance camera by the grave. "Only that historian will have the gift of fanning the spark of hope in the past who is firmly convinced that *even the dead* will not be safe from the enemy if he wins."[8]

Abu Nidal's red cap has a conspicuous white rectangle where he had removed the Coca-Cola logo. He described himself as a communist, then corrected himself, saying with a laugh that he was "an organic communist," explaining that *perestroika* was a terrible idea. Uncomfortable serving tea upstairs in the formal lounge room, he took us downstairs where, surrounded by construction equipment, he liked to talk and set the world in motion. Down there he makes his own cigarettes which look factory-made with little gold crowns on the shaft, and down there he feeds his newborn birds, each the size of a thumbnail. He had recently broken his arm but instead of going to hospital set it himself.

The situation cannot last long, he says. No colonial power has ever lasted, and when the people in all those ridiculous Arab states around us really rise up and overthrow the corrupt systems dominating them, then all will change here too. No state based on religion can last because it is inherently racist.

What a surprise to hear that his family includes people of Russian, Italian, and Japanese descent. Images of "ethnicity" and purity crumble. And here he was, the "organic communist," more worthy as a role model and recipient of a Nobel Peace Prize than any politician with a National Park named in their honor.

His "park" is a little smaller. Surrounded by an electrified fence and with a tunnel under the wall to the grave of his ancestors resting in the peace of an Israeli surveillance camera, should his park not receive recognition, too? I can imagine Israeli kids and Palestinian kids camping there in the summers within the safe confines of the fence gathering walnuts in the Abu Nidal Organic Communist Park.

***Thursday:*** In Palestine more than anywhere else I've been, dates are critical benchmarks in time that sculpt present reality: the 1948 war, the 1967

---

8. Walter Benjamin, "Theses on the Philosophy of History," in *Illuminations: Essays and Reflections*, ed. Hannah Arendt, trans. Harry Zohn (New York: Schocken, 1968), 255.

war, the first intifada of 1987–1993, the Oslo accords of 1993, the second intifada of 2000–2005—along with the dates of the demise of marriages and communism. A friend tells of how as a kid she experienced the first intifada in Ramallah with its roilling enthusiasm and excitement, the way people in the West today recall 1968. The front and back doors of the houses were kept unlocked so people could run through and escape the soldiers in the street. If you kept those doors closed the community would come down on you. She recalls being awakened by strangers running through the corridor. There was a boycott of Israeli goods by the stores. School was held in people's homes. The university closed and classes were held in the street. And a continuous presence of Israel soldiers. But the second intifada? A farce, she says. A feeble copy of the first because Oslo, meaning the Palestinian Authority, compromised everything. It was not a "popular intifada" but part of a larger political game that had to do with Arafat's machinations with Israel. The world plummeted: the USSR collapsed (1991), The Gulf War took place (1991), Oslo was signed(1993), and her parents left the communist party and divorced.

*Friday*: "Shall I continue? Shall I go on?" It was a moment in which everything changes into the timelessness of "this can't be real." We were on a ridge outside of Bethlehem. A white sedan was diagonally stationed in front of us across the narrow road with tall trees on either side. Just beyond were two humvee-like vehicles with soldiers clambering out, opening the back, seizing trumpet shaped rifles. Then they stood still paying no attention to us. "Border soldiers," she said. "The worst." Silence. "Shall I go on?" The car in front nosed its way between the two military vehicles and we followed it. There was a loud *ka-thump*, the sound of tear-gas guns firing one hundred yards behind us and a canister came awfully close. "Roll up the window!" Not even enough time for fear. Around the corner peered a group of kids like in a cartoon, only it wasn't, girls leading the boys, some with stones in their hands. They were from eight to twelve years of age. We sped on.

*Saturday:* I receive an e-mail from the young woman—the anthropologist Amahl Bishara—involved in the youth center in the camp in Bethlehem. "The sad news from here," she writes, "is that Mohammad Al-Azza, the man who took you around and who was injured in the face, was just arrested in the middle of the night yesterday by the Israeli army. It was an especially violent raid, with dozens of soldiers in their house. Mohammad's parents, uncles, aunts, and cousins were all beaten—three went to the hospital—and he was beaten as well. It looks like the arrest is because of his photography work, though we won't hear official charges for a few days. No one can be in touch with him now (except that one meeting w/ the lawyer, which I think he was lucky to get). So that is rough." [9]

"So that is rough." I rack my brains trying to think of what I can do, paralyzed by anger, dismay, and no options. Only yesterday, or was it the day before, I was sitting with this man drinking coffee with the sniper's tower visible above his left shoulder as if we were on a stage set with the cameras ready to roll. Only it was no stage set. It was magical realism for sure, only the magic was very sinister.

A friend in the US who works a lot with photographers responds to an e-mail I write him, asking me what do I have in mind when I suggest some response is required. It is an unanswerable question. He says that the story "is all over the Internet" and that it is well known that the IDF targets media people. I feel impotent. Being "all over the Internet" seems in today's world not only a way of removing something from sight but instant death of the spirit and imagination, which reminds me of the many e-mails I have received, ending with "have a great time in Palestine."

Another friend suggests I check out *Maan*, a Palestinian news agency online that among other things documents the many depredations of the Occupation. I scroll down and down and down some more until the facts become lost in white noise.

I try to place myself in the shoes of people back home in the US dealing with everyday issues, the heat, buying groceries, job anxieties, family rituals, whatever—like Marlow in *Heart of Darkness* vainly trying to get across to his listeners in England how impossible it is to convey the reality of the Congo. "You can't understand," he says. "How could you?—with solid pavement under your feet, surrounded by kind neighbours ready to cheer you on or to fall on you, stepping delicately between the butcher and the policeman." [10]

**Sunday:** In the hills above a Palestinian village near the university of Birzeit, thirty minutes from Ramallah by car, there is a huge Israeli settlement on the ridge lying opposite a huge Palestinian refugee camp spreading down the slope. All the contradictions are here piled on top of each other, a stone's

---

9. He was released after ten days' imprisonment.
10. Joseph Conrad, *Heart of Darkness* (New York: Penguin, 1983 [1902]), 85.

throw apart. Sameer's friends' parents live lower down the hillside in a two story modest home of concrete and stone painted a soft brown which they built a few years back, now surrounded by almond trees, fig trees, plum trees, flowering aubergine, tomatoes, onions, and other vegetables. It was late afternoon. The father was on his knees tending his plants and the publisher mom was lying in a tiny pool not much bigger than a bathtub watching him. Sameer explained that the father had been a militant years back but since then has dedicated himself to this precious garden. The mom published children's books but gave up because the Israeli state made it too difficult to export books out of the West Bank which has too small a market to sustain publishing. She tried to set up publication of her books in Beirut and Amman, but the costs were prohibitive and she eventually found a job with an NGO in Cairo. With that salary they were able to build this little house. Visiting from London was her daughter with her husband who works there in human rights and is in Palestine investigating the killing of a thirteen-year-old boy shot in the back by Israeli soldiers for breaking through the infamous wall. Soldiers are instructed to fire with real bullets if their lives are deemed at risk.

As the sun set around 8:30 we walked up the hillside with a flashlight to inspect a newly found ancient grave, unearthed by bulldozers digging the foundation for a neighboring home.

Three meters above the ground, suspended on stones, was a stone slab about five meters long and thirty centimeters thick. At ground level was a square opening barely large enough to allow a human body get through. Some adorable puppies were playing by it. Four gangling boys aged about fourteen appeared and in Arabic explained there was strange writing, not Arabic, on the wall inside. Without hesitation they wriggled into the aperture and Sameer followed with the flashlight.

When he emerged a few minutes later, two young men in their early twenties appeared out of nowhere and began talking with him. They came from the nearby camp, and were plenty scary. "Who's the chick?" they demanded, pointing to our artist friend. "How much does she cost?" They had, they said, five friends hiding farther up the hill.

Were they drunk, as Sameer thought, or on drugs? Sameer, who grew up in a camp himself, asked them their family names, the presumption being (as he later explained) that knowing their names at once established an connection and a caution, if not a counter-threat. The puppies kept playing with the gangling boys at the entrance to the grave as we retreated down the crumbling hillside, sliding through the thorny underbrush.

I realized how unusual till then had been my stay in Palestine where I walked the streets of Ramallah without a worry as to my personal safety any hour night or day. I got to thinking it must one of the safest cities in the world in terms of assault and theft, and Bethlehem likewise. Locals confirmed this impression which, after my many years in Latin America, seemed unbelievable. It was as if all the violence of which people are capable, generally speaking, was absorbed by the one vast violence of the Occupation (and, as someone was quick to point out, the corruption within the Palestine Authority).

But I did hear of the existence of Israeli and Palestinian mafias from a British geographer working in Ramallah. The Israeli mafias sell the arms they acquire from Israeli soldiers to their Palestinian counterparts. A brilliant one-state solution.

**Monday:** Looking over my notes I am troubled by the absence of any mention of economic class. For many years I had naively, if not unthinkingly, assumed that all Palestinians were in some profoundly important sense a unity which obliterated distinctions by class. But, of course, nothing could be further from the truth. Simply look at the cars in the street or at the houses where the differences leap out at you. More to the point, this economic difference can have serious implications for political negotiations with Israel and the US, it being to the benefit of rich Palestinian businessmen to strike a compromising deal so they can make money in ways that may not really benefit anyone else. That gets to the root of the rot so many people with whom I speak feel about the Palestinian Authority.

**Tuesday:** It was dusk. She drew the car to a halt in the driveway of her long absent parents' home in Ramallah. In the strange intimacy of that moment with the car, but not the conversation, coming to rest, we hesitated to get out and she continued, her voice halting. "I told them how I was not a virgin and that I was living with my boyfriend in another country. For a whole year they refused to talk to me. For a year! I would call but they would hang up. My sisters say, "Why tell them?" but I figure it is more respectful to tell them." Gesturing vaguely between her legs she bit her lip saying "My vagina is everyone's business."

After a pause she said, "Actually I live under six occupations."

The first is my family
The second is my community
The third is the Palestinian Authority
The fourth is the Israeli Occupation
The fifth occupation is the swarm of NGOs in the West Bank
And the sixth is global capital.

**Wednesday**: Caro insisted we visit Hebron because she had such searing memories of the place from a visit the year before. Ala nodded, as if he knew what she meant. "Micro-ethnic cleansing," he said.

Standing on the roof of a Palestinian office building in the Old City of Hebron, we could see the stony hills surrounding. On each there was an Israeli military base, three in all, and, in addition to the standard Israeli strategy carving up the West Bank into three areas A, B, and C, I was told there were additional subdivisions operating within the city itself—H1 under Palestinian Authority control, 80 percent of the city, and H2, the remaining 20 percent under Israeli control, reflecting its divided and tense character as a religious center of staggering importance for Muslims and for Jews and thus a microcosm of the conflict as a whole.

Why is this city of such sacred importance? In part because of its foundational role for both Muslims and Jews in the figure of Abraham who is buried here. In part it is also sacred because of massacres. In 1929 sixty-seven Jews were massacred and in 1994 a New York–born Israeli-American settler, Dr. Baruch Goldstein, stormed the mosque during Ramadan killing twenty-nine people at prayer with a machine gun and wounding some 150 others. The crowd killed him.[11]

Since 1967 the mosque housing Abraham's grave has been divided into a mosque and a synagogue. The centerpiece is the replica of the tomb of Abraham. Covered with a green cloth with gold embroidery it is visible through iron grates on its mosque side and also from the synagogue side, although the view from that side is partially obscured by a sheet of bulletproof glass.

Inside the mosque is dark, high-ceilinged, and relaxed, with deep, cool shadows. Kids play while in a corner some dozen women sit in a circle, taking instruction from a woman teacher. On what? "Oh, marriage and men and women . . ."

---

11. In 1999 a monument to Baruch Goldstein in Kiryat Arba was destroyed by the Israeli army because it had become an extremist shrine.

To get to the synagogue section of what before was all mosque, I have to walk past concrete barriers and soldiers. The synagogue is brightly lit and overflowing with books in Hebrew. Men in black suits and black hats sit isolated from one another reading as if their lives depend on it, as I guess it does, nervously rocking the upper body forward and backward while others seem to be praying as they read, the soft whispered voice giving bodily expression to the primacy of the printed word. There are few children. The women stand in the back and as a group rock back and forth while praying, each one with her own book.

I see a text on the wall which I take to be unintentionally allegorical, purporting to document the stealthy transgression into the mosque by Israelis searching for the holy of holies, the cave deep in the earth containing the remains of Abraham and that sweet soft fragrance of the Garden of Eden itself. It reads like a dream, a most disturbing dream, surreal and cinematic.

## Entering the Cave of Machppela by Noam Arnon

*Following the return to Hebron, Jews desired to reach the actual caves of Machppela, buried deep beneath the huge Herodian structure.*

*Defense Minister Moshe Dayan, an amateur archaeologist, tried to seek information concerning the underground caverns. Within the large hall, called the "Yitzhak Hall," under a brown monument, there is a hole in the floor. This was rumored to be an entrance into the Caves of the Machppela themelves. However, the diameter of the hole was extremely narrow—twenty-six centimeters. No adult could possibly fit through this opening, but Dayan found a solution. A twelve-year-old named Michal, young but courageous, agreed to be lowered into the underground room.*

*One night in October, 1968, Dayan ordered the Muslim guards to leave the building. Michal was brought to the site. The opening was uncovered and Michal was lowered into the underground room. . . . Dayan wrote out the findings and sketched the underground caves.*

*Thirteen years later a further attempt was made. As the area was always occupied by "Arabs" preventing further access, we began saying special prayers of repentance every evening at midnight. The Arab guards, employed by the Waqf, the Muslim religious trust, left and went to sleep. Seeing this we brought with us a big chisel to the midnight prayer service. In the middle of the service, we began to sing and dance. During the dancing, some of us made our way to the Arab prayer-rugs, lifted them, and revealed the stone. It was held in place by metal bars. . . . Suddenly we felt a breeze, the cave deep in the earth. We found bones and pottery—dated about 2,900 years old from the era of king Solomon and the Judea kings . . . by the entrance to the Garden of Eden where souls and prayers ascend.*

In the street outside a middle-aged, paunchy man with an old red backpack was shouting. The soldiers refused to let him pass to talk to our Palestinian guide's father who had one of the few remaining stalls with tourist knickknacks including brightly colored fabrics hanging from the ceiling. The middle-aged man trying to pass worked for an Israeli Human Rights organization and his every move and that of the soldiers was being videoed by a colleague as with exquisite slowness he made his way forward inch by inch, as more soldiers with guns arrived. A settler in a white minivan drove slowly by, laughing, then turned around and passed once more. Our guide's father was shouting too, as if holding a public discussion with both the human rights worker and the soldiers. "You think you're king!" he thundered at the soldiers. From the other side of the street, the human rights worker shouted his questions to the guide's father as part of his interview. Half an hour later I saw him inside the stall with its fluttering fabrics. Dwarfing this tableau stood the vast building containing Abraham's tomb, penetrated by Moshe Dayan, chisel in hand, dancing and praying, lowering the flower of Jewish girlhood deep into the earth of Palestine in a wildly transgressive assertion of primordial rights.

To one side of the vast building that is Abraham's tomb there are blocks of deserted "Arab" homes and shops that settlers had annexed, block after block. Nobody could be seen in the street other than a few soldiers. A ghost town. Another movie set.

At the end of an enclosed passageway nearby, with stalls selling spices and food, the sky once again became visible, except for a ceiling of wire mesh. Why? Because now and again, so I am told, settlers occupying the houses throw garbage onto Palestinians passing below. The town wanted to roof over the space for protection, but were forbidden by the IDF, so I am told, as that would obstruct the soldiers' view of the Palestinians below buying vegetables and spices.

Days later I was told by a new friend that she had spent the day with villagers whose fields had been swamped by sewage from an Israeli settlement. Deliberately, she thought.

**Thursday:** Every night that I went to sleep in Bethlehem, knowing that a brilliant sun would wake me early, pouring through the blindless windows into my large white bedroom, I thought of the owners who must have slept in this very same bed before fleeing to the US during the second intifada (2000–2005). Nobody lived in this large house on a steep hill except for one of the daughters. The high-ceilinged rooms downstairs were dark with the shutters closed all the time, emitting a sad empty feeling of absence you could cut with a knife were it not for the grace of the daughter like a flame illuminating the shadows, the shadows of exile. Washing lay in piles on couches upstairs as if the final task of storing them in closets was just too much. Next to the closet in my room were two bullet holes from the intifada, the others having been covered over.

"Thank you for connecting to the invisible — for not sleeping in a room without honoring the spirit of those who lived in it, for not looking at my abandoned laundry as mere reflection of neglect, yes, it is a task too much to do . . . to put away everything in the closet, to declare in such an action that all is well, that everything is organized, that the people are coming home. . . . I don't think anyone is coming home anytime soon and that is perhaps the hardest reality to digest and why this wash is still laying here weeks after your departure."

*Intifdada?* The word is generally taken to mean "uprising" or "awakening"; more literally "to shake off, as a bird shakes water off its feathers," or, as I was once told, "to beat a carpet"! Ignorant of Arabic, I am struck by its wealth of metaphor, polysemy, and verbal associations. I guess this sensation occurs when encountering any language for the first time, awakening that alertness to metaphor largely lost to a native speaker in the same way, as Nietzsche pointed out, that the emblems on a coin become dull through usage. Maybe so. But this awakening to image and metaphor in a foreign tongue lit my way and was a constant delight.

My guide had a preternaturally keen eye for birds flying high in the sky, dots disappearing into the blue. What do you call them in Arabic, I asked. *Abusaad*, she said, Father of Happiness.

# The Go Slow Party

*The time is past when time did not matter* [1]

*We will travel not only in space but in time as well.* [2]

---

1. W. Benjamin quoting Paul Valery in "The Storyteller."
2. William Burroughs, *The Letters of William Burroughs, 1945-1959*, edited and with an introduction by Oliver Harris (New York: Penguin, 1993), 58.

## I. Agitada

I knew it was all over that morning at my desk when I got an e-mail complaining I did not stay in touch enough. I know life is sped up, she wrote, but nevertheless. . . . I forget the rest because the word she used was not "sped up" but *agitada*, a word that made me shiver with recognition, *agitated*, a word uncommon in English, a word that stuck like a *dagger* in my heart as well as in the heart of things in a cruel, cruel, way, for what is at stake, what is actually, secretly, at stake in the great speed-up that second by second assails me and—I imagine—you too, is that this one word so powerfully transmits the craziness of the speed-up oscillating back and forth like a compass needle seeking magnetic north or a tiger stalking in a cage, tail flicking in rage and torment. I then realized that along with global warming, the speed-up is the principal form the state of emergency takes in my time, only I normally don't see it that way because it sneaks up on me step by step. But one day out of the blue as with hurricane Irene and the evacuation of New York City you realize how insane life has become and that without a revolution in time, humanity is doomed.

Of course, there is one usage not uncommon in English: *the agitator.*

Before I got that e-mail, the speed-up that assails me second by second and—I imagine—you too, was something that filled me with leaden despair in direct proportion to the galvanizing call to move, and be damn quick about it too, as when faced in the morning by a mountain of new (I was about to say "fresh") e-mails. What *agitada* did was displace that leaden despair with an electric probe. But how can I possibly describe this restless state, propelled by fear and inchoate desire?

The worst thing about the speed-up is that you should not betray the slightest sign of anxiety. Of course everyone complains that life is going to hell through speed-up and overload. But are they serious? Our whining is like white noise. No one is really going to do anything drastic. As with the weather, everyone's complaining but nobody is doing anything about it. In fact complaining is part of the ritual of ever-readying readiness, so long as it is merely a pause, waiting for that second wind so you can rejoin the marathon. Get with the program! Pull your weight. Don't be a wuss. Go fast, young man. And, let's face it; nothing can stand in the way of progress. It is like climate change or worse. Save your breath. Time is money.

## II. A Little History of the Beach

But do you remember how it used to be in the morning, that time when you got straight into creating crisp, crackling, sentences, aflame with incandescent thought? Do you remember?

Do you recall the days on the beach as a kid, making tunnels and sandcastles, following rivulets of sea water swirling through seaweed and periwinkles stuck fast to rocks? Truly then was the time when time did not matter. Time was a periwinkle stuck fast. Time was rivulets of sea water.

As we got older we learned to body surf, immersed in the surge of the wave. It was the wave that did the work. We would float out "the back," as we called the smooth zone beyond the breakers, and chat and chant and call out to the gods of the sea to send us a big smooth translucent green one trembling at its peak.

We would play hooky from school—from work, that is—and hitchhike to the beach. What a feeling of freedom, of going slow, that was, to combine strike action against school with lying on the hot sand staring into the endless blue of the radiant sky.

And what a wonderful Go Slow feeling it was—I kid you not—to stand in the dust by the side of the road hitchhiking. You could wait a long time but that in itself was bliss. That was the time when time did not matter.

Later came surfboards and something fundamental changed. Surfing became work. Those surfers did not look especially happy scooting back and forth on the wave. In fact they looked quite grim. They did not loll about playing like seals immersed in the sea. No sir! Last time I was at Avoca there were tents and loudspeakers dominating the beach. There was a board-riding competition for money.

Sport became work, faster, competitive, "no pain, no gain." I saw a sign by the road yesterday. *Ride the Ridge: Bike Challenge.* And the forest was full of large yellow signs with black arrows for people racing reach other on their bikes. Forget the humble walker. No wonder I haven't seen an animal there in years, but then yesterday I came across a small tortoise on the path. Its brown shell was studded with golden hexagons like badges of honor.

## III. Colonizing Play

This little history of the beach from childhood to adult, from back then to now, from walking to racing, from challenge to tortoise, raises the point that not only have we lost the beach and the periwinkles stuck to rocks with salt water sluicing, but that many if not most things that look like Going Slow such as cycling and surf boards actually involve work and speed. What has happened is that Going Slow has been colonized by the Go Fast economy. The art of play has been converted into something that looks like play but is actually a means for making work work, defined by instrumentalism and the profit motive. This is a far cry from the idea of unproductive expenditure.

A whole opening up spreads its wings at this point. To contrast play with work is to problematize the meaning of both. It is to feel their co-dependence, the ways they feed into one another as much as they oppose each other and disintegrate in each others' grasp. This is the wondrous achievement of the Go Slow Party, that deterritorialization of work and play.

Thinking back to the child with sea water sluicing as an epitome of Going Slow, it seems to me that the basic contrast with work is that of living within things versus manipulating them from the outside. The former implies a mimetic desire for empathy and a capacity for becoming Other, while the latter implies the opposite, a wrenching apart from the world so as to better manipulate it. The former implies a yielding relation to the world, a mastery of non-mastery, while the latter colonizes that in order to master the world.

It was in America, a restless, driven nation of work and speed, that I was asked by a waiter in a restaurant if I was still working on my food.

All this makes you wonder about the meaning of life. Yet how naive and embarrassing this question seems today, "the meaning of life." Indeed, how revolutionary! For what is meant is more than a question. It is a cry for a new art, namely the art of living. What will it take to transgress the prohibitions against Going Slow when—as my friend Carolina Trigo puts it—each of us today is our own little market economy?


## IV. The Right to Be Lazy

Much ingenuity will be required, she notes, to retake one's body and inhabit time. Who was the more perceptive in this regard, Karl Marx or his son-in-law, Paul Lafargue, author of *The Right to Be Lazy*?

The first copy I had of Lafargue's book was in Spanish. I bought it in Cali, Colombia, in the early seventies. The cover displayed a person lying in a hammock. Years later in the nineties I put up a Colombian hammock in my office. Deirdre de la Cruz, a new graduate student, entered the room and gasped. "We should have these in the library," she exclaimed. At that time my university department was changing to a postcolonial outlook, meaning an academic confrontation with colonialism and the ways it has affected the discipline of anthropology. Our office space was being redesigned, and there was discussion about what to do with the lounge. Following Deirdre's remark I suggested we outfit the lounge not in chairs and sofas but in cotton hammocks. After all, what could be more postcolonial—the medium is the message—than reconfiguring human posture this way? But my efforts were fruitless. There were many fine talks and classes about the evils of colonialism but the furniture could not be changed which, when you think about it, as an anthropologist, must surely include the furniture of the mind. After all, what does a body in a hammock do?

Swinging in space = Swinging in time

Suspended

As the earth rotates

In his essay on art in the age of mechanical reproduction, Walter Benjamin pin-points an obvious yet unremarked knowledge. This is our sense of our bodies in relation to space, especially to what we could call intimate space. Such knowledge informs the deeper layers of habit and plays a fundamental part in maintaining, or changing, social conventions.

In a lecture on what he called "techniques of the body," delivered about the same time as Benjamin was writing his essay, the anthropologist Marcel Mauss outlined a field of study comparing the way people in different cultures walk, swim, dig, sleep, stand, and so forth.

Emanations of the bodily unconscious, it does not seem far-fetched to me to suggest that what is at stake here is the connection between the body and time—think of swinging in a hammock—that endorses ways of life. That is why there is all the difference in the world between sitting in a chair and sitting cross-legged on the ground or lying in a hammock. And this why Proust called his book *In Search of Lost Time* precisely because of his concern with the making and breaking of habit, as the young Beckett emphasizes in his little book on Proust.[3] Our postcolonial critics sit in chairs, not hammocks, as did Karl Marx with terrible boils on his bottom. But Proust? He wrote interminably long sentences that played

---

3. Samuel Beckett, *Proust* (New York: Grove, 1957).

with time branching like ivy on old walls and he wrote in bed through the stillness of the night where body and time become one. It was there with his interminably long and convoluted sentences sensuously exploring sensuousness that he slowed down almost to a standstill our procedures of perception, re-constellating both the bodily unconscious and our habits of attentiveness.

Yet is not speed essential to the attentiveness of reading (and writing)? Benjamin writes that the semiotic quality of language becomes mimetic thanks to the speed with which we scan the words on the page. Yet this mimesis is self-limiting, to say the least. In fact it is ephemeral—which is what gives meaning to meaning and enables language. The semiotic quality of language, writes Benjamin, provides the coherence through which, "like a flash, similarity appears. For its production by man—like its perception by him—is in many cases, and particularly the most important, limited to flashes. It flits past. It is not improbable that the rapidity of writing and reading heightens the fusion of the semiotic and the mimetic in the sphere of language."[4] Hence, we might say, there exists a strange kinship between a written text and a movie, presumably an avant-garde movie.

Does not Benjamin invoke this same long lastingness of the mimetic flash in his primer on revolutionary thought ("Theses on the Philosophy of History")? At several points he rests everything on the attempt to retain a memory as it flashes up at a moment of danger, noting that "the true picture of the past flits by." (What sort of movie would that be?)

## V. The Mastery of Non-Mastery

It often seems to me that people need something to push against in order to exist and feel real, and that what we call "the economy" has taken enormous advantage of this. We have become psychologically programmed to exploit ourselves such that every moment is but a step toward something else and hope springs eternal in the human breast. I call this the "anti-gravity rule," more commonly referred to as "alienation," by which I refer to something like the Old Testament story of Genesis, that after expulsion from the Garden, men and women were cursed to live by the sweat of their brow. Normally this is taken to mean that you have to till the stony soil, grow crops, and make shoes, wars, and babies, etc. This means that man-

---

4. Walter Benjamin, "On the Mimetic Faculty," in *Refelections* (New York: Schocken, 1986), 335–36.

kind is plagued by the curse of not being able to do nothing and has to continuously push against gravity. Hence the "anti-gravity rule" fundamental
to what Hegel called "negation."

A terrifying, even masochistic, proposition, this is also the foundation
of Hegel's allegory of master and slave in search of recognition and self-
consciousness through the gaze of the Other. For reasons that are far
from clear, one person risks death and becomes the master, while the
other does not risk death and becomes his slave, yoked to work. (Perhaps we should understand this as not given in humanity so much as an
account of history in which humanity keeps on changing, but then how
many masters have actually risked death, their own, that is?) Basic to
the outcome of Hegel's just-so story in which the slave achieves mastery
over the master is *praxis*, meaning the interaction between self and the
inner life of things as we might find with work—or with art and with
craft (including the craft of the storyteller)—such that a more or less
continuous feedback loop or, rather, a spiral, is formed. The idea here
is that the worker but not the master shapes external reality just as the
shaped external reality shapes the worker who shaped it, and so on back
and forth. "Shaping" is perhaps not quite the word here as it suggests
external transformations when what is intended is what we could call
an "organic" interaction with the inner life of things even though history
has yet to facilitate such interaction other than exploiting that inner life,
such that work remains boring and meaningless, a primary cause of a
stunted humanity and an ever more poisoned environment.

Hegel's master-slave allegory finds masterful interpretation and expression in filmmaker Joseph Losey's film *The Servant* (scripted by Harold
Pinter), in which the male servant to a rich young man idling his time
in posh London gradually achieves power over his master; partly on account of his well-honed skills at cooking and cleaning, anticipating his
master's every desire, his wonderfully dignified obedience—his thought-
ful care and concern, just this side of intimacy—and, as time goes by,
both his and the master's skills at sexual adventure, misadventure, and
the downward vortex of the joys of mutual destruction.

What Hegel's "negation" actually musters is a restless anti-gravity rule
taken from Bataille's playbook that continuously undoes both master and
slave, opening up the possibility of the mastery of non-mastery which I
take to be the magical password to the enigmatic art of Going Slow.

## VI. Yielding to the Life of the Object

In particular the mastery of non-mastery involves the particular.

Mastery of non-mastery is built on resistance to abstraction and tilts toward sensuous knowledge which perforce includes desublimation of the concept into body and image. At times, albeit rarely, Hegel is adamant on the need to "return" to the sensuous particular away from the abstraction, as in *The Phenomenology* he unleashes an aberrant untamed writhing of negation, saying that nowadays "the task before us consists not so much in getting the individual clear of the state of sensuous immediacy . . . but rather the very opposite; it consists in actualizing the universal and giving it spiritual vitality, by the process of breaking down and superseding fixed and determinate thoughts" (94). True scientific knowledge, he says, demands yielding to the very life of the object. Knowledge needs "to seep itself in its object" and "be sunk into the material in hand" (112).

"Yielding to the very life of the object."

Is this not the art of the mimetic faculty?

Can we surmise, therefore, that to Go Slow is to be mimetically sunk in the material at hand, like the child's hand sluicing sea water, a hand many times removed from Adam Smith's "invisible hand" regulating the exchange of commodities galvanized by the abracadabra of abstract value? Can we further surmise that this aversion toward abstraction acts so as to transform Marx's "exchange value," mediated by the Universal Equivalent of money? If so, then to Go Slow would mean changing the meaning and function of money, maintaining it as a medium of exchange but curtailing its metamorphosis into capital. This is not a step backward in time to so-called precapitalist economies, but a step forward, taking advantage of the fetishism of commodities, rerouting the animism therein such that the sea water sluicing the child's hand flows into the body as it meets the body of the world.

Bataille writes of different political economies of excess, his focus of attention being on the way economies spend the surplus by means other than capital investment, exemplary of which is the festival and potlatch. It is logical, therefore, that so much of his work concerns religion, which he conceives of as the attempt to overcome the alienation from things created by work.

## VII. Speaking of Slow: A Few Days Ago

I e-mailed an anthropologist friend Lisa Stefanoff, long resident in the central desert of Australia, and told her I was trying to write a Go Slow Manifesto calling for a Go Slow General Strike as the next step beyond Occupy, appealing for a new civilization (manifestos tend to be a little loony). I wrote because I had a dream about two old friends in Sydney, one of whom is very ill.

"Great to hear from you," she replied.

*I was beginning to think you'd been swallowed by something hungry with big teeth. Call her Uni admin? I despair of this work myself, barely doing any real research or writing or reading, it seems, on account of the administrivia. I have a beautiful pressed tin sign on my wall, something I found in Bali, that says Slow Down. Can I please join your movement and start the Australian chapter? Growth, what a disgusting global paradigm. We ain't evolved for it at this speed. And joy music love food sex walking swimming sleep talking are so much more slowly important . . . I'm almost out of range, tapping in iPhone in troopie as we head north but this is a new camp for next two years. Lots of love from us all, dogs included.*

Two days earlier I received this e-mail from another old friend, Carolina Trigo, which I have edited slightly:

> Hey mick
> i've been pondering on this for a while, hopefully my observations don't come too late :-)
> but i find myself living this question right now.
> what does it mean to live slow and what are the implications it opens up in terms of choice, autonomy and co-habitation?
> From personal experience: I went far to the north where you feel Slow almost immediately.
> The change was dramatic. For the first time in a long time I felt i was re entering my body, and felt peace devoid of the incessant head-ramblings of "you should do this or that and achieve this and that."
> That fear, that sense of anxiety or success—which was really one sense . . . the sense of "making it"—dissipated between the trees in the forest and the reflections on the lake. so simple and so epic. so quiet and vibrant.

I felt (and still feel) that in that regard the country I was in some sort of outcast utopia.

and of course, it led to me a crisis.

cause there is no change without crisis, or is there?

some moments:

I met a man and he took me to his cabin by the lake. We took a long boat ride close to sunset, rowing. He's so quiet and as I was observing him or rather my relation to him, asking: what makes that silence, how is that held?

I looked around me and saw the wind moving the trees, the openness of the lake, the speech between us which was really about glances . . . and i realized that his sense of silence was not too different from the landscape we were in.

open, still, observant. Gave me an inkling into a way of life I had forgotten.

and i kind of fell in love with that.

the notion that life can be something other than the incessant pursuit of something else. that it's about being present.

Which leads me to some thoughts:

the main question to me is: how does slow become a choice, a way of life? and how is that sustained?

Does slowness require being / becoming an outcast?

which implies:

an autonomy of Slow / or a Slow autonomy

The de-privatization of co-habitation

courage and responsibility

questions of relationship and distance between:

comfort and peripheries.

being and speed

Virilio says "speed robs us of our duration." I love that. That's the loophole. This culture of speed is the culture of success. We have become our own little market economy, we consume our own life in the pursuit of happiness.

These e-mails have given me much to think about, particularly the nerve that has been struck by the idea of Going Slow.

## VIII. The General Strike

In the occupation of Wall Street in October 2011, itself a splendid example of the festival, I come across onlookers laying down their cameras and backpacks so as to pedal bicycles generating power for the occupation. One woman sees it in historical terms running in matrilines. As she pedals, smiling, she says, "I can tell my grandchildren I provided energy for OWS." By her side a bunch of older women sit sedate in lounge chairs knitting woolies for OWS, subverting, at least symbolically, the commodity. They are the epitome of Go Slow, dwarfed by the towers of Wall Street where speed is of the essence. They have all the time in the world for they inhabit time and time stands still. They don't need to explicitly reference history or the matriline. They are all that, composed of what Benjamin called "the time of the presence of the now"—the mysterious *Jetztzeit*—which, truth to tell, is not time at all but events and memories freed of their moorings. Clickety-clack go the knitting needles as the very idea of history is re-constellated. The women have cardboard signs by their side voicing their outrage. Clickety-clack. This is not the clickety-clack of the locomotive of history which Marx invokes in his preface to *The Introduction to the Critique of Political Economy*. This is not even the clickety-clack of Benjamin in his anarchist (Blanqui) mode, trying to figure out when to pull the emergency brake on the train that will usher in the revolution. Nor is it the explosion that Benjamin invokes as the blasting apart of the continuum of history. Revolution is different now.

What I have in mind is a Go Slow General Strike that, with Sorel and the Wobblies in mind, would be based on making explicit the question, What Are We Living For? What Is Life About? Once we've got the money out of the hands of the rich and the bankers and the real estate and energy moguls, once the one percent have had to pay their debts to society, we will realize that's the easy part and only the first step. What lies ahead is changing work and time, including control over what one is producing and why one is producing it.

With the Go Slow Party, work is no longer a commodity sold to the highest bidder. In other words, because it enters the heartland of labor, Going Slow entails radical communitarian politics concerned with capital investment and productivity. Going Slow is at once philosophical, economic, and political. And like Marcel Mauss's and Malinowski's characterization of the gift as an alternative economy, neither capitalist nor communist, this new practice of time will be aesthetic and magical. It is a plea to step aside from the juggernaut and rethink what it is to be human in the world by dismantling the time machine, more dangerous than the war machine to which it essential (see Virilio).

## IX. Going Slow Includes Going Fast with Sudden Ruptures in Time

The Go Slow Party is not all slow. It is like a butterfly on a hot summer's day. It speeds up and slows right down to alight on something interesting or beautiful, making it more beautiful. Think of Benjamin's "flash" of similarity in Proust's languor. Like a butterfly the Go Slow Party is also erratic in flight—unlike the speed-up assailing us all which is demonically torrential.

Without its own forms of speed carefully knitted into its being, Go Slow can be suffocating, as with the crushing boredom that afflicts people who work in offices the world over, a favorite subject for Franz Kafka, and surely one of the great evils of modern and not-so-modern history, an offshoot of what Max Weber referred to chillingly as "the iron cage." With dread and despair I recall the zombie-like faces and lizard-like posture of the clerks awaiting the five o'clock closing time in the Land Reform Institute in Bogotá several years ago. Like tailor's dummies they sat at their desks examining their fingernails or shuffling papers from one pile to another. Walking through such spaces is to smell death. To escape from that form of Go Slow to the consciously chosen bed-ridden Go Slow situation of Oblomov, the bureaucrat in Goncharov's Russia, is to experience salvation.

Going slow in the shower this morning I thought that the only time I really go slow is in the shower and having a shit. Both are fine examples of what Hakim Bey called "the temporary autonomous zone." Both free the mind and stimulate creative thinking combined with what Lyotard called "drift" in which floating, freeing, meditative, moments flow and fold their dreamy selves into sudden insights—and then more dreamy selves. Both indicate in the clearest of terms that what we call consciousness is in fact a wide spectrum of activities of mind between being asleep and being awake.

This pattern of dreamy nonchalance punctuated by sudden rupture is a fundamental expression of the speed-up necessary to going slow. Such is the way, if way it be, of what Bataille called "unproductive expenditure," mainstay of what he came to call "general economics." Going Slow would learn from and expand on these quintessential moments of the daily round, rooted in the particular, where infrastructure meets superstructure and structure dissolves. Going Slow in present-day society would be a festival of time combined with a festival in time in which the heterogenous time of the exception—the *jetztzeit*, as Benjamin called it—displaces homogeneity.

Of course there are many everyday instances of this and we should each of us think carefully about them for the clues they provide for the Go Slow General Strike. (This is the technique Michel Leiris uses for getting at the sacred in everyday life.) I am thinking of the examples in the e-mails that my friends sent me that I quoted above, and in no special order other examples occur to me such as traveling two hours in the bus from New York City north into the countryside late at night, falling half-asleep, lulled by the vibration. Swimming provides similar moments which swimmers call "the zone." To stare at the wall or out the window while writing is to also inhabit the temporary autonomous zone or TAZ, as students call this enchanted space. I assume joggers get into the same zone, but this raises the question of whether "fast Go Slow" is really Go Slow or colonization of Go Slow?

Walking in the mountain but not so much the city parks has traces of this too, time off from the business of the world. Walking in the streets of the city, however, is quite the opposite technique, immersing oneself in the business of the world so as to be free of that business—as portrayed by Walter Benjamin with his idea of *colportage* mixing the experience of hashish, the montage of cinema, and walking in the city.

All these activities require doing something physical in order to do nothing, or doing something in order to do something quite different, which is what Benjamin has in mind with not only telling a story but listening to it as well. "Boredom is the dream bird that hatches the egg of experience." I recall the women knitting during the Occupation.

Go Slow can be a weapon. I recall the sloth I saw on the wharf on the Pacific coast of Colombia. It barely moved. It was the archetype of the Go Slow General Strike. Its claws were like razors. Similarly that tortoise I saw on the mountain, can bite off your finger (so I've heard.). In the sheerness of its sloth, decrepitude has something of that too, being a barb directed straight at the heart of the work world. Beckett's characters have this, as does Barnaby the scrivener. Here, to Go Slow is to register the Mute Absurd of contemporary existence.

These examples combine speed with Going Slow but the quality of the speed is different to the speed-up which chokes life, just as the Going Slow is different to the enforced slowness that grips unemployed people the world over. In the shower and on the can, Going Slow provokes speed— meaning the eruption of an idea. Sleeping on the bus tearing through the night combines speed with stillness, space travel and time travel. Whether on the mountain or in the streets of the city, walking involves flow and cessation as in Benjamin's comment on the state of emergency as "not the exception but the rule" which, characterized by slow, ever-increasing compression, may of its own accord usher in a revolutionary explosion. This same dynamic is expressed where Benjamin writes of thinking itself as a stop-go process which "involves not only the flow of thoughts but their arrest as well," and it this that provides the paradigm for the return of the Messiah, meaning "a revolutionary chance in the fight for the oppressed past"—which takes us back to the time when time did not matter.

This anarchistic vision of revolution as speed and rupture is commonplace. What is less frequently acknowledged is the Go Slow phase which is not merely the necessary preliminary but also the sequel, that of paradise or utopia.

## X. Agitada

I am teased continuously about working so hard on my Go Slow Manifesto. The phone rings. It is my daughter. She wants to know if the Go Slow General Strike means I can't wear my *Speedo* swimming costume anymore? And will we have to stop swimming butterfly and only swim breaststroke? She is taking time off from her work—her endless work—drawing stark wastelands for her animated film. She is way behind her deadline, an ominous word now neutralized by usage. "Don't give me a line. Give me a deadline" (Duke Ellington).

Imagine a world without deadlines. Would anything get done? In the old days it was the coming of winter, spring planting, birth and death and the slave driver's whip that got people off their arse. Nowadays you do it to yourself, master and slave in one.

As I write this talk, in stops and starts, I see professors walking to work, head down, back bent, they seem sad and broken yet think they are free.

Actually, it's worse than that, for the speed whipped up by the deadline acts as a stimulant. Many of us like—or think we like—the speed-up. We even think we need it. We love the challenge (a common expression). We want to compete with time and win. Bring it on! Adrenaline for the soul.

But once I got that e-mail and saw that one word—*agitada*—the game was up. It was magic, like in Brecht's poem about fear in the Third Reich in which the fortress crumbles at the pronouncement of the one, magical word.

The idea behind that poem is that power relies on bluff to keep us in line but because bluff is itself magical—at least imageric and performative—it can be laid low by apotropaic magic, as with that word *agitada*, redolent with cosmic discord.

It is no accident that the e-mail which set me thinking—this *agitada* e-mail—was sent by a person without a computer, living in an agribusiness plantation town in western Colombia suffering mightily from the speed-up otherwise called economic development. The first phase was in the 1960s with the displacement of a leisurely peasant tree agriculture by exhausting wage labor in the sugar plantations now producing biofuel for cars. The second phase was when the state created a tax free zone for light industry with twelve-hour shifts of young girls on assembly lines night and day. And the third phase occurred the past fifteen years with the replacement of manual labor on the plantations by machines imported with state subsidies. Along with this came drugs and gangs, cocaine, fast motorbikes, beauty and sex and murder—all in all, a mighty speed-up, and no doubt this is merely the beginning.

The tiger stalks in its cage, tail twitching.

# Iconoclasm Dictionary

**A: Antiquated:** Why does iconoclasm seem so dated? Are there no more icons to smash? Of course there are the Stars and Stripes flying proudly over every secondhand car lot, gas station, and fast food outlet, which strikes me as especially transgressive but somehow is not considered to be so, not like in the good old days when people would wear the US flag on their butt or burn it to make the Great Communicator mad and compel scrutiny by the Supreme Court of the land. Today it seems the world has gotten divided between places begging for a little bit of iconoclasm and those where iconoclasm has lost its bite. Truly protest has gotten harder in the Western democracies. Along with kettling by police of mass demonstrations and erection of chain mail fences closing off targets, as with the G-20 protests in Toronto, so-called free speech and free markets allow everyone to be an iconoclast and yet search in vain for a target he or she can get close to. That in itself, of course, is a belated sign of success; that the forces of law and order have to expend such spectacular military force to stop iconoclasts, and yet it must make the bankers and politicians feel grand as well and compete with one another for bigger and brassier security details. Of course what's important here is that even in this digital age, iconoclasm must mostly be a physical affair with the human body in close proximity to the icon. It seems that no amount of ferocious blogging or vile online anonymous commentary can even get close to the impact of human bodies marching down streets or tearing down a statue. How strange, you say, that even today the human body could assume such presence! Could it be that the power of icons as much as of iconoclasm depends on this presence made intimate? And what could be more intimate than destruction? This would explain why icons suddenly burst into consciousness and themselves seem to come alive only with their defacement. You smash them and, lo and behold!, they have become icons. This back-to-front logic is of a piece with the rhythm of taboo and transgression, attraction and repulsion, that runs through all societies and all of social life. Even in good old days—especially in good old days—icons begged for a little bit of iconoclasm because their aura owes much to the curious ambivalence of taboo because what endows an icon with its respect also demands its defacement. When the prime minister of Australia, a politician not especially fond of Australia's allegiance to Britain, touched the queen's butt many years ago, what an uproar. He said it was an accident. Well, so what! But that butt had been crying out for a touch and, what's more, in being touched, accidentally or not, its iconicity soared. Iconoclasm is written into the icon. Taboos are meant to be broken. Well, that's how it used to be anyway. In the good old days.

**S: Sacred:** Now, however, it seems something strange and wonderful has taken place. Before there was a discernible distinction between sacred and what Bataille following Durkheim called "the negative sacred," meaning something so ghastly that, profane and profanating as it might be, it nevertheless generated a great head of *sacred steam*. Examples? Incest. Bestiality. Use of menstrual blood in sorcery. A widely respected rabbi in Washington, DC, secretly taking photographs of Jewish women undressing for their ritual bath. Secretly closing off the traffic lanes to the George Washington Bridge out of spite. Etc. (Note, a lot of secrecy.) But now it seems like transgression itself has become the new sacred. Is that possible? It was complicated enough before. But now? Oh, my God!

**I: Icons:** Icons used to be icons. You could spot them a mile off, maybe on a pedestal or accompanied by a brass band, touching the sky with bird droppings all over—not like shop and bank windows, shiny surfaces with stuff to buy on the other side, along with all the bellyaching that goes on these days for transparency. When the arcades were built early in the nineteenth century, which Walter Benjamin made the object of his study meant to rouse Europe from the death-sleep of capitalism, there were no shop windows in the streets nor display of things for sale. Icons were really icons in those days. You could spot them a mile off.

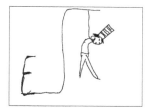

**E: Effigy:** I recall in decades past seeing photos of effigies set alight in public protests in Third World countries, especially of Uncle Sam with a stovepipe hat and striped breeches. But that seems long ago. A strange-sounding word— *effigy*—it recruits magical powers through pronunciation as much as anything else, especially powers of hate and destruction that despoil the copy of what is to be hurt, a process that Sir James George Frazer of *Golden Bough* fame called "sympathetic magic." This is the ground zero of iconoclasm, cheap, brutal, and nasty, like smashing the shop window. Very satisfying, I imagine.

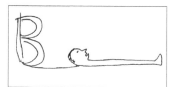

**B: Body:** The human body can be an especially potent target of iconoclasm as witnessed recently by the young vendor in Tunisia who set himself aflame, providing the spark that sent the dictator and his cronies scuttling. Before that this humble street vendor was not an icon. Before that he was anything but an icon. It needed self-immolation to make him one and he will be remembered for a while, maybe a year, maybe less, and songs will be sung and poetry recited and his photo held aloft. When I wrote this in late January 2011, other Middle East dictators propped up by the US were in serious trouble because of this. The Egyptian government was tottering. In late 2014, videoed beheadings by ISIS of prisoners in Guantanamo garb jacks up even further the iconicity of the human body.

**W: Wikileaks:** Is secrecy an icon and revelation iconoclasm? Is it not amazing that one of our best sources of insight into the background of what is even now, in 2015, happening in the Middle East, comes from leaked diplomatic cables? Who or what is the icon here, Julian Asange, private first class Bradley (now Chelsea) Manning of the US armed forces, stewing in solitary confinement, or the US government? Since then Edward Snowden has revealed secrets that beggar belief. The current rage on the part of the US government and the baying for blood by some US congressmen testifies to the battle being fought over this question, the real icon being the sacred nature of state secrets.

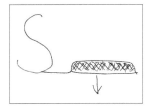

**S: Suicide Bombers:** These are iconoclasts supreme. Yet it is strange how their action has become routinized and they are now seen more as bombers than suicide bombers. James Scott wrote a memorable book called *Weapons of the Weak: Everyday Forms of Peasant Resistance*, making me ask whether suicide bombing is one such weapon, a sign of desperation in the face of a highly mechanized enemy such as the Israeli army or the US and Canadian armies in Afghanistan that put massive resources into protecting the soldier's body? But surely suicide bombing is not just another weapon of the weak, a matter of fox-like Brechtian cunning? The moral element in any act of iconoclasm is stupendously brought forth by self-immolation. It is thus extremely important that we in the West take note of how the media has set a de-iconoclastic tone such that suicide bombers are now just bombers. This happened with great speed.

**N: Nietzsche:** As for the moral element in any act of iconoclasm, how might we first think of the value of destruction that the larger than life mid-nineteenth-century anarchist, the Russian, Mikhail Bakunin, called a creative passion? In *The Gay Science*, Nietzsche has a paragraph, "We Destroy Only As Creators" which seems like the other side of the same coin.

**S: Sacrifice:** This is confusing. Nietzsche calls attention to self-immolation as the weapon of the weak to dominate the strong. Think back again of the young man setting himself aflame in Tunisia. Christ is an archetype of humility and *resentiment*

is the term Nietzsche uses for this performance of abjection. But on the other hand—and it is a very big hand indeed—sacrifice is the supreme act of prodigality, of giving for the sake of giving that Georges Bataille, follower of Nietzsche, called *depense* of which sex and sacrifice are the great examples. Sacrifice consecrates that which it destroys, writes Bataille, while Marcel Mauss and Henri Hubert also emphasize that the victim becomes divine. How much greater does this becomes when self-sacrifice is involved?

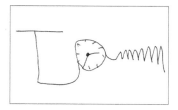

**T: Time:** Is iconic, just try being iconoclastic and have your own time like the Greek I met in Athens who boasted how he never kept to the time of appointments but turned up whenever he felt like it. Nothing would bring the modern world to a halt more quickly—certainly more quickly than torching police cars or breaking bank windows. In his "Theses on the Philosophy of History," Walter Benjamin distinguishes homogenous time from heterogenous time. The former belongs to clock-time and to the idea of progress. But heterogenous time, which he also called the "time of the now," is a sudden rupture in time when something in the present unexpectedly leapfrogs over time so as to constellate with something in the forgotten past. There is a cessation of movement, a strange nothingness out of time and here it is when the Messiah may return—in other words, a revolutionary chance in the fight for the oppressed past. "Thinking involves not only the flow of thoughts, but their arrest as well." Benjamin refers us to holidays today as sad vestiges interrupting the flow of time with traces of this other time, the time of the now. He thinks of the calendar as a monument of such forgotten historical consciousness. In the July Revolution in France in 1830 there occurred an event which showed this consciousness to be still alive. On the first day of fighting several different clock towers were fired on simultaneously. Time stood still.

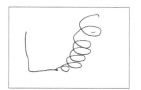

**L: Lightning:** Foucault is fascinated by what I call the back-to-front logic of taboo and transgression of which iconoclasm is an example. Along with Bataille he is not phased by the fact that transgression merely suspends the taboo. Both philosophers instead direct our attention to what Benjamin calls the "now time," the *nunc stans*, of the heterogenous time opened up even if only momentarily by iconoclasm. Neither of them mentions Benjamin, who actually attended ,with some incredulity, it seems, some of the sessions of the Collège de Sociologie in Paris in 1938–39 where the taboo and the sacred came in for a lot of heavy lifting. But there is a remarkable convergence of thought here. Along with Bataille, Foucault thinks language fails us at this moment. Bataille writes of thought jumping the rails, of how when the very heavens open we can speak in nothing but clichés. Foucault, however, becomes positively rhapsodic at this incapacity to speak and lets fly with a torrent of heightened language a lyrical hysteria in which the very impossibility makes the speaker redouble his or her efforts to express what is happening but keeps slipping though his or her fingers. There is first a lot of geometry in an effort to show how infinite is the experience, the experience of iconoclasm, meaning the experience of the paradox in which each step of rupture or of breaking the taboo results in yet another taboo and the effort multiplies, feeding on itself. (This is an interesting, even mystical, feature of iconoclasm, I suppose.) Hence we hear a lot about spirals rather than breaks or ruptures, "the form of a spiral which no simple infraction can break." We hear of circles too, but not your smooth circle. Instead it is a circle made of "fissures, abrupt descents, and broken contours." It is a "misshapen and craglike language" folded back on itself and continuously questioning its limits. Then there are the cosmic and meteorological metaphors in which iconoclasm is likened to "the solar inversion of satanic denial," or to "a flash of lightning in the night which from the beginning of time, gives a dense and black intensity to the night it denies . . . yet owes to the night the stark clarity of its manifestation." The reason Foucault writes in such breathtaking manner in my opinion is because he is doubly stressed compared with Bataille. It is now maddeningly complex. Bataille may have been a proto-postmodernist, but Foucault is the real thing and for him there is after the Death of God no solid taboo to butt against such that transgression itself becomes the new god and as such takes the form of sex which, as he insists, has to be spoken about in order to remain a secret. Oh, my God!

**D: Death of the Author:** They say you should always keep an author separate from his or her text, that it is quite wrong to allow biography into literary criticism. Some go further and talk of the Death of the Author and, as did Barthes, relate such death to the songs of shamans acting as mere vehicles for a sacred or magical text. Yet I cannot not think about authors; of Foucault as not only gay but for much of his life, at least, as in the closet, just as I cannot not think of a gay activist in Uganda beaten to death with a hammer in late January of this year (2011) for being gay. Can we really say there are no more taboos? And what happens when gay sex becomes no less tabooed than straight sex? Sex is always tabooed, right, even in marriage?

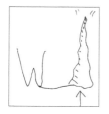

**W: Wisdom:** Why is it that wise-sounding people are quick to tell you that iconoclasm actually boosts the iconic power of the icon and thus betrays the iconoclast? There is so much joy in destroying the icon and even more, it seems, in destroying the joy the iconoclast enjoys.

**O: Obelisk:** Some societies have permanent sites for iconoclasm. This is worth thinking about. Like the sea, iconoclastic waves batter against this Supreme Being, only to fall back again as the Supreme Being rises intact or stronger than ever. Such is the huge obelisk in what came to be called the Place de la Concorde in the center of Paris; but before it got that name of Concorde, it was the site of the guillotine during the French Revolution where Louis XVI and Marie Antoinette were beheaded. Now, that's iconoclasm for you, beginning with the name *Concorde*! Perhaps we can call this *sacrifice*, but in any event what to me is eye-opening is the layering of history, from the guillotine to the obelisk, from the king to the republic, and in particular the unconscious or barely conscious manner by which myth and magic converge in creating a permanent site of Concorde for iconoclasm such that suddenly—like the human body set afire in Tunis—the history and magical power of the obelisk can, on iconoclastic occasions, leap out at us. Weighing 250 metric tons and being seventy-five feet high, there seems as much magic—technological and statist—entailed in its transport from its home in Egypt, as there was in its original purpose in Egypt which seems tied in with the worship of both the sun and the dead, mindful of the name given Louis XIV as "the Sun-King." Two mighty states, the theological state of Egypt and the Republican one of modern France, converged in forming what is surely the ritual center of the French state and where the German Army set up its headquarters in WWII. In 1993 the AIDS activists of Act Up managed to unroll a pink condom covering the obelisk. We always knew the obelisk existed there, surrounded by snarling traffic. But once the pink condom was in place, then the obelisk truly came into being. As an illustration of what he meant by the "dialectical image," Walter Benjamin in his *Arcades Project* cites Chateaubriand (born 1768) who wrote about the Obelisk de la Concorde, "The hour will come when the obelisk of the desert will find once again, on Murderer's Square, the silence and solitude of Luxor" (p. 399).

**A: Animism:** Is there a career or life history to an iconoclastic act? If so it might go like this. First the stage of invisibility or taken-for-grantedness of the icon. Then the stage of its destruction or humiliation, which automatically leads to the third stage, that of resurrection, as the icon explodes into visibility because of aforesaid destruction or humiliation. It is no longer taken for granted. It has burst into consciousness, not only in its damaged, destroyed, or humiliated form, but also, in memory, at least, as it was before its disgrace when it existed in its noble, pristine, pre-traumatized form. Sometimes there comes a fascinating fourth stage, the moment of animation in which the damaged icon comes alive in a most disturbing way as objects are not supposed to have life like this, bred of violence and death now mixed with sacred or magical emanations. If this is true or true enough, then it seems a terrible simplification—an impoverishment—to say that iconoclasm paradoxically increases the power of the icon. Yes! Agreed. But so much more is going on. When Neil Roberts felt moved to pick up the damaged statue of the Queen of England, along with her consort, the Duke of Edinburgh, decapitated and amputated, and place them in his pickup truck and take them to an undisclosed location, he seems to have felt that something unbearable had occurred. "It's gone beyond a bit of fun now," he said. In their destruction the statues had come alive.

**C: Contagion and Proliferation:** There is another stage as well, more like a flow, and this is that once iconoclasm has occurred, it is like pulling a thread in a stocking such that the whole thing can unravel. Foucault's spirals come to mind. A person who breaks a taboo, for example, is likely to be an object of dread, full of some evil toxin which can spread to other people. Freud specifically refers to this as contagion in his book on taboo. AIDS was like this the first few years, and still creates a chill, same as what is now happening to Muslims in the US with the congressional hearings organized by an IRA militant, republican party stalwart Peter King, who endorsed terrorism in Ireland and now endorses the use of state terrorism which, of course, spreads the contagion of fear.

**C: Castration:** This is a quote from a news source:

> A phallic phenomenon was short-lived after police told a 16-year-old boy to remove a snow sculpture emulating male genitalia from his front yard on East River Street and Yale Avenue. Roman King said it took about 20 minutes to shape the 7-foot sculpture about two days ago. He said he created it "just to see what people would think," and he has gotten "car honks with people giving us the thumbs up," from drivers while it was standing. "My friends really like it," King said. But after police came by Thursday afternoon and told King to remove his interpretative model of the male sex organ, he said this was the last such sculpture he was likely to make. —Ohio *Chronicle-Telegram*, http://tinyurl.com/4c2smnl.

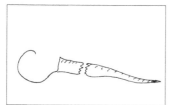

It is hard to say what is more iconoclastic here; building the phallus in the front yard or making the sculptor tear it down. Then we have to consider his name, *Roman King*. This quotation has some strange wording, such as "emulating" as in the "snow sculpture *emulating* male genitalia," and "interpreting" as in being made to "remove his *interpretive* model of the male sex organ." On the one hand, it seems that the mere act of imitating is to run the risk of exceeding reality in a morally disturbing and even exciting manner, especially when it comes to the phallus. On the other hand, we have the safe harbor of cognitive relativity with the introduction of the notion that any representation is merely an interpretation. Yet surely what is disturbing about the phallus is that it is the very model of the icon and of iconicity? What does it mean, then, to make an icon out of an icon, of the mother of all icons? I recall a brilliant colleague in Ann Arbor explaining to me many years ago Charles Sanders Peirce's trichotomitzation of the sign into the icon, the index, and the sign proper or symbol. As I recall his explanation, the icon is evoked when we speak of a phallic symbol such as a skyscraper—which is, he said, iconic on account of the shape. So why don't the police order skyscrapers razed? Why don't motorists honk when they drive past a skyscraper? Could it be because the skyscraper is actually an index and not an icon, an index meaning that there exists a cause-and-effect relationship between the phallic drive to dominate on the part of architects creating new fangled obelisks? As I recall further it all got dreadfully confusing because having trichotomized so neatly, Pierce then went to say each category contained elements of the others. No such thing, therefore, as a pure icon? Where does that leave iconoclasm? Ask Roman King.

# The Obscene in
# Everyday Life

*January 1, 2007*: My twenty-two-year-old son rents a video from Kim's
by the name of *Clerks 2*, telling me that *Clerks1* was pretty funny, and we
sit down to watch it around 8:00 at night, the night before he returns to
school. He explains that it is a sort of documentary, showing the lives of
people who clerk in stores like a 7/11 or a McDonald's in New Jersey, a place
that to the enlightened people of Manhattan epitomizes obscenity anyway, full of SUVs, suburbs, chemical plants, and people too cheap to live in
the city but come to Manhattan weekends to indulge in strip clubs, fancy
restaurants, and Broadway shows. Well, after a few minutes we are pretty
disgusted; there is not a line of dialogue without reference to genitalia
or lurid sexual activity, the movie drawing to a close with a fleshy bald
male called Kelly in black leather long johns sucking off a donkey on an
improvised stage with a smoke machine in what looks like a McDonald's.
"It's disgusting," says one of the young women in the movie referring not
to McDonald's but to the size of the donkey's penis offscreen, "but I can't
stop looking." Georges Bataille could not have put it better with his mantra,
of attraction and repulsion. Is this the genius of the vernacular? That it can
express convoluted highbrow ideas in a pithy phrase enlarged by the mise
en scène? Bataille's other term, made much of by Julia Kristeva, namely *the
abject*, also springs to mind, a troublesome term that to me suggests a close
kinship with the obscene—note the strange prefixes at work here, *ab*ject
and *ob*scene and start to plot your etymolygies. This movie, I say to myself,
must be a particularly revealing instance of so-called *popular culture* which
I always feel I am missing out on and don't really know what it is. Once you
have bracketed it like that and given it a name, "popular culture," I fear

you have already lost it. Could the same apply to the obscene? Thank God I have this son of mine who knows popular culture inside out and when home from school acts as my guide, as did the pagan Virgil to Dante, lost and confused, making his way ever deeper underground to the nether parts of the Devil himself on his way to redemption. They say it's adults who educate children, but nowadays it's so obviously the other way around, at least when it comes to *popular culture*. When I was a kid in Australia in 1952 I went to see a locally made movie called *Bush Christmas* in which two friends of mine from up the road, Nicky Yardley and his brother Michael, starred. What a thrill it was to see the credits flash on and see "Adults Only Permitted if Accompanied by Children." The film concerned a handful of children, boys and girls, outwitting a gang of bushrangers. How crazily innocent it all seems when viewed from today with movies like *Clerks 2*! What has happened in the intervening years, along with everyday reports as to child abuse, widespread hysteria concerning so-called sex offenders stigmatized as loathsome beasts, and prepubescent girls acting like sex kittens as depicted in that wonderful movie *Little Miss Sunshine?* Which of these categories of behavior deserve to be called *obscene* and which do not? This question is made all the more complex by the fact that in *Clerks 2* the obscentities—if that's a fair epithet—are so terribly natural, unstressed, unexcited and unexciting, like someone asking for a Big Mac or a Coke, in which case, why bother? Why the autistic lack of emotion re the obscene? Is this the new sitcom, sex without sex? Could this be the ultimate sanitization of society, de-eroticising the erotic?

*January 2:* Downtown Manhattan in a bar waiting for my other son. I am thinking of writing something for this obscenity in Iowa conference and am pondering how much the Western world has changed with respect to the moving line separating the obscene from the non-obscene. When Thomas Hardy got his most celebrated novel, *Jude the Obscure*, published in England just over one hundred years ago, it was greeted with shock at the attack on marriage, class, and sexual mores, meriting a review entitled, *Jude the Obscene*. In *Sister of the Road: The Autobiography of Boxcar Bertha* (by the anarchist obstetrician-gynecologist and lover of Emma Goldman, Ben Reitman), Bertha tells us of her beloved mother's father, a farmer in Kansas (not that far from Iowa) who, in the 1880s, was one of the organizers of the free love convention at Worcester, Massachusetts. This man served three terms in jail, two of which were for sending birth control information through the mail, which the federal authorities called obscene. And regarding this moving line separating the obscene from the non-obscene, isn't it a curious fact that I find it difficult, if not impossible, to define one or the other of these terms outside of their coupling as mutually antagonistic opposites, same way as Emile Durkheim defines the sacred, as not the profane? I am early so I sit by the bar after locking my bike outside on Sixth Avenue where I notice a bearded, muscly guy in his forties dressed in black looking like Kelly from the movie last night, sitting outside this cold early evening by a lonely table smoking a cigarette and talking avidly into the cell phone cradled in his ear. A far cry from the haunts of the bridge and tunnel crowd from New Jersey, the bar has yet to fill up with its usual crowd of yuppie bohemians and academics like myself. A man and woman are sort of making out seated at a table by the window, looking pretty glum. Three or four guys are at the bar talking chummily with the barman. A young waitress tying on her apron takes my order and over a glass of red wine balanced on a tiny copper topped table I try to read my novel, *Distant Star* by the Chilean Roberto Bolaño—"the most influential and admired novelist in the Spanish-speaking world," according to Susan Sontag. I notice a camouflage-patterned backpack hanging over the chair next to me. Immersed in the mysteries of the strange poet, or is he a spy?, in the time when Pinochet took power in Chile, I fail to notice the entry of the bearded muscleman from outside, sans cigarette, who, despite there being plenty of empty seats, sits down right beside me speaking loudly in an *Oh! I am so gay!* manner of speech into his cell phone, so loudly and with such flair that you had to wonder if actually he wasn't talking primarily to the few people in the bar for whom the supposed person at the other end of the phone was merely an excuse. "So we went to the hospital," he booms, "and she's gonna have . . ." and he opens a note book and slowly reads out, syllable by syllable, "palliative treatment." "This is good," he goes on to say in a voice at once cajoling and authoritative, a voice that brooks no dissent, as he describes what happened yesterday, what happened today with the lung tissue slides at Sloan Kettering, and how all of that connects with what will happen tomorrow with the ambulance to White Plains. I am sitting there like an idiot unable to shut out this saga. It seems like the other person on the phone never speaks (isn't it *always* like that with cell phones?), pulverized by this monologue and perhaps by grief and anxiety. It is sickening to be exposed to this intimacy, the intimacy of death, no matter how anonymous such dying might be in relation to the captive audience in the bar, and I have little hesitation, although I do have some, in designating this activity as obscene. The hesitation I have has to do with the way people often refer to something they dislike as "obscene," thus injecting moral condemnation where it doesn't seem to quite fit. This is puzzling to me and its delineation might shed light on the meaning, today, of obscenity. To offer what might not be the best example of what I have in mind here, let me recall a strange moment in which a graduate student was giving a talk, accompanied by slides, on the eating clubs at Princeton, his talk being billed as one of those rare occasions where the secrets, or should I say sociology, of the rich and privileged are to be revealed. This was according to the senior professor, exemplar of Nietsche's idea of *ressentiment,* whose disgust of the rich and powerful was equaled, I suspect, by her desire to become one of them. Her protégé, of similar disposition, chimed in when, the question was raised whether it was ethical to show the faces of the Princeton students photographed? Someone proposed that maybe the faces could be masked in some way, causing our protégé to blurt out with a voice of thunder brooking no dissent, "That would be truly obscene," a statement I remember as vividly as if it was yesterday. Turning this over in my mind, as has been my wont at unexpected moments over the years, I keep wondering why this would be thought of as obscene, indeed "truly obscene," and frankly I have no answer. What I do feel sure about is that all of us in that room were with that remark being marshaled like sheep to pass into a scary place where one was to be morally strip-searched and, worst of all, we had no idea what we had done wrong. In other words, it was not the suggestion as to masking and making persons anonymous that was obscene, "truly obscene," but that rejoinder itself—suggesting that those who would designate something as obscene are playing with fire and may well turn out be more (truly) obscene than what they rail against. The very category, the word *obscene,* comes alive and bites the hand that feeds it. In other words, the line dividing the obscene off from the non-obscene is anything but clear, anything but stable, and, what is more, is such that even to name it, even to mark it, is to run the risk of adding to obscenity's mysterious power and fall victim to its stigmatizing effluvium. But enough of this madness and back to the bar on Sixth Ave. where, having finally laid his phone to rest, the bearded man—obviously a favored customer, perhaps a waiter himself or even the manager—calls over one of the young men waiting tables and in an even louder voice than on his phone says, "Hi Mark, you're the worst sex I've ever had in my life." Not even Bataille with his marked interest in the confluence of sex and death could have predicted the perfection with which his theory would manifest itself as it did that second day of the New Year, 2007. I pack my bag and take Bolaño's *Distant Star* to a table as far away as possible in the back room aglow with Christmas lights.

*January 3:* Now that I've got this idea of an "obscenity diary" I am training myself to be more conscious of obscenity and am wondering why this heightened state of awareness so interests me. I am now in a more activist mode, fine tuning my antennae as to the obscene instead of just waiting for it to happen. Three years back Jimmie Durham sent me a copy of his nature journal that he kept for many months in Berlin and I thought it wonderful, matter-of-fact whimsy concerning the odd bird that makes its appearance toward the end of winter, some new grass by the canal, the character of the frost. What made it charming was the basic idea that nature in the city is a fascinating topic, like an illegal immigrant hiding out between the artificial splendor of the well-ordered parks to one side, and car exhaust, on the other. But it is the cast of mind that's important here—not so much what one is looking for, but the way one looks—as when Jimmie writes his entry for December 24, 2000, about buying a wild goose, cooking it, then the first snow of the year falls around five in the evening, everything becomes white and quiet, and he goes out onto the small terrace and hears a crow calling in the distance. This sense of nature as antithetical to the city as a wild intruder is surely analogous to obscenity with its necessary affinities to what is deemed right and proper, reminding me of the story I was told by my late British anthropologist friend Olivia Harris in the 1970s of how surprised everyone was when the British government built one of its first motorways, the M1, and instead of fleeing, the rabbits returned to the edges of the motorway and built their burrows there, apparently enjoying the vibrations. Is that rabbit analogous to obscenity? Once conscious of my new mission I start seeing obscenity everywhere. In the swimming pool today there is this really fat man who looks so obscene in the shower with his tummy falling over his thighs and black hair over his back like a wild animal. Swimming he looks like a whale having a seizure. But now you have to be careful because fatness is not a laughing matter, what with juvenile diabetes, largely caused by fast food joints such as the one in *Clerks 2*, and fatness has been dignified as a civil right and McDonald's breathes a little easier. Anyway aren't we each and all free agents, responsible for how we look and what we eat? I ask myself, What would Jimmie's diary have to say about this nature in the city? Leaving the pool I get on my daughter's bike and pedal through Central Park. It is a fine day. People are happy. In fact it is too damn fine, almost a summer day and it is the middle of winter. The radio tells me that 2007 will be hottest year ever. The planet is in trouble. My dentist chuckles over my gaping mouth. She has a sunny disposition and can be very funny, an advantage, I would think, for someone who has to look down into cavity-riddled mouths and wobbling tonsils all day such that it becomes routine. Well, maybe not quite routine, which is where a TV program like MASH gets its humor, mixing the devastatingly serious—some would say "sacred"—surgical opening of the human body by scalpels and retractors combined with the routines of the operating theater including wisecracks and distractions such as playing opera during long operations, same as William Burroughs's famous "routines," he called them in his letters to Alan Ginsberg, concerning Doctor Benway throwing scalpels and swabs around in gay abandon. Not quite so funny are my memories of medical school, of the year we students spent in small teams of four or five students dissecting the human corpse, one team at the top, head and trunk the other team below when, to my horror, I was told by a friend that that one of our fellow students, a star athlete, was cutting out part of the female genitalia from several corpses and keeping them in a matchbox. We are used in anthropology to the concept of "licensed transgression," those occasions societies set aside, such as initiation rites or Saturday nights, when the rules of decorum are relaxed or transgressed, by permission, as it were, thus making of transgression a complicated business indeed, partly rule breaking, partly rule conserving. In such a situation is obscenity truly obscenity, and what then of unlicensed transgression as with the scalpel wielding medical student whom none of us informed on? "Well," my dentist says, probing tooth Number Eighteen, "we ruined this one (meaning the planet Earth), let's move on to the next!" "And everyone laughing and enjoying the sunlit end of the world," I say between opening and closing my mouth. And she laughs too. She is very smart and can understand even when I speak with my mouth full of probes and such. When I rode to the dentist through the park, black nannies in droves were pushing white babies in baby carriages under the pines that the wealthy people on the Upper East Side have donated. A black man sat playing a drum with a small coat on the ground for coins. He was still there two and half hours later when I pedaled home, playing the tom-tom for the white folks. Opposite the Metropolitan Museum of Art a mammoth stretch limo black and shiny suddenly pulled out.

Could have killed me. Parks illegally and is still there when I pedal, motor exhaling carbon monoxide, the driver barely visible behind the dark glass of the window in his suit and tie peering into a small computer as his boss gorges on art. Thinking about the history of the Louvre, in one of his more memorable Surrealist pieces for his famous dictionary in his 1930 magazine, *Documents*, Georges Bataille suggested that the art gallery in our time has taken over the sacred site in the center of the city that was the king's palace. The story goes like this. When the king was beheaded in public during the French Revolution, so the city's abattoir, also in the heart of the city, awash with blood and offal, was moved to anonymous locations outside of the city and people could then enjoy their Sundays of purification by going to the art gallery while the obscene roots of the sacred in the sacrifice of the king and animals is nowhere in evidence. Well, almost so, because there is in fact startling evidence of unruly emotions afoot when you consider that within a few years Napoleon placed in the same square in Paris where the king was executed the lofty obelisk he took from Egypt. At first sight what we brusquely reduce to the name *Enlightenment* provides a useful tool for organizing these events with the sacred giving way to art, Napoleon, and imperial booty. But then does not the "counter-enlightenment" swing in, and with a vengeance? Art has become the new sacred, the abattoir is the repressed shadow of sacrifice, and the king's head has risen to new glories in the obelisk. It is a lot of fun to point out these reversals and unexpected connections that work behind men's backs, but the essential point is my use of the words *obscene* and *sacrifice* as when I write of *the obscene roots of the sacred in the sacrifice of the king and animals*, because (a) it is jarring to consider that the sacred is obscene, and (b) that the execution of the king *and* of animals in these historically specific situations can be considered to be sacrifice.

Bataille wrote this short piece on the Louvre and the abattoir almost eighty years ago and while the general idea is as relevant and as riveting as ever, there are other sacred, or should one say *negatively sacred*, sites that undergo the same disappearance as Bataille's abattoir. I am told, for instance, by a mechanic friend in upstate New York that none of the towns in the vicinity allow junkyards, which he calls *salvage* yards, to be exposed to the public and they have to be situated outside of the towns. The county town planner and the local town clerk inform me that local laws demand high walls around such yards which must be on the outskirts, never inside, the town, and the same applies to strip joints which are not allowed to have blue lighting on the outside. In town planning parlance strip clubs are called "adult uses" and fall into the more general category of LULUS, meaning Local Unwanted Land Uses, which includes slaughter houses as well. No prime space on Fifth Avenue like the Met for them! No wonder that a mom in Texas got confused recently when her ten-year-old was taken on a public school outing to the city's art gallery in Dallas and came home talking of statues of naked women and as a result the art teacher was fired. What are naked ladies doing in the center of town? The small town of Rosendale near where I live upstate, a town with a population of roughly five thousand, two hours north of New York City, had a plan drawn up by a Republican councilman (who was also chief of the Fire District) for the creation of an industrial zone—"park," I think he called it—which would destroy many beautiful acres of what remains of the forest by the river and this, he added earnestly, would be just perfect for "adult uses" as well. So is this the new sacred geography of America, walled-off junkyards with gutted motor vehicles alongside windowless sex clubs (I mean "adult uses") with low ceilings and dark lighting forming along with the slaughter houses a ring of outposts around the perimeter of what passes for a town center of gas stations and convenience stores selling lottery tickets? As I cycle back through the park, the sun is setting and it is getting nippy. The black nannies are wrapping up their charges and heading home. Some tourists are taking photos of the sun visible through the spaces left by the skyscrapers to the southwest as foregrounded by the trees of the park. The contrast is overwhelming. This is the New York sublime, better than the Grand Canyon. In front of me on a beat-up dirt bike an elderly man, Hispanic and poor-looking, is leisurely cycling, hunched over the handlebars. From somewhere invisible on his person or his bike, enchanting music is pouring out real loud. I mean *really* loud. It sounds like Coltrane and in this setting it is beyond all expectation and stereotype which is why, I think, the gaggle of uncomforted-looking Upper East side folk sitting on the benches admiring the sunset, like me find this obscene, yet sacred too, and don't know what to do.

*January 4, 2007:* Many years ago as Europe took the first steps toward the Holocaust, Bataille's collague, Michel Leiris, gave a blessedly short talk to the Collège de Sociologie in Paris as his contribution to what his Surrealist colleagues were calling "sacred sociology." He called the talk, "The Sacred in Everyday Life," and after running through memories of his childhood, such as the mysterious yet familiar glow of the stove, *La Radieuse*, in the kitchen, his father's silver-plated revolver, secretive bathroom antics with his brother, and children's games with language, Leiris concluded that the sacred was not restricted to formal situations such as rituals of the church but existed as living force in everyday life, the mark of which was danger, ambiguity, mystery, and the unexpected surprise or shock we might associate with the Surreal. This account differs remarkably from the notion of the sacred set forth in 1912 by Emile Durkheim in his famous work *The Elementary Forms of the Religious Life* in which the sacred was designated as a feeling of awe, reverence, and fear associated with something set firmly apart from the everyday which he designated as the *profane*, a confusing word that means both mundane or ordinary as well as the negative sacred. Leiris challenged or seemed to challenge this distinction of sacred and profane by locating the sacred in the profane, granting the sacred a light and playful character, but Bataille went further in emphasizing the obscene basis of the sacred, no less than the sacred basis of the obscene. Little more than a footnote to Leiris's sacred in everyday life, my obscenity diary displays, I believe, something important to this montage effect of purity coexisting side by side with impurity by having them run one after the other in daisy chains of uneven yet daily occurrence that tear at our logic no less than our language. Why I have chosen a daisy-chain mode of production of narration combined with an ethnographic diary I am not sure. Could obscenity lend itself to such chaining, or enchainment, and if so could that be because it produces an excess of emotion and thought associations that evoke still more in a veritable fountain of excess? Does obscenity throw a monkey wrench into repression beginning with the repression that goes into sentence connection and grammar? Am I practicing an obscene mode of literature, or ethnography? And as regards the ethnographic diary approach, Wittgenstein is an encouragement. He talks about our talk and wonders out loud about our apparent confusions and contradictions but most of all about our senselessness—of which we are blissfully unaware—especially when we adopt the high road of the meta-level and ask unanswerable questions like, What is the Sacred or What is Obscene? Leiris spotted this dilemma too, for dilemma it surely is because these questions are as important as they are unanswerable. In my hubris I have extended Wittgenstein and Leiris by writing little scenes or ethnographic sketches with each one serving as a comment on the one preceding, searching for a medium that can perhaps do justice to the unsayable no less than the unsaid.

# Syllable and Sound

"The brain is just the weight of God," wrote Emily Dickinson,

> For, lift them, pound to pound,
> And they will differ, if they do,
> As syllable from sound.[1]

Poets must be shamans of a particular kind, playing with language, which means playing with interpretations, tricks of reference, and heart-rending ambiguity. It is a tremendous thing, the ultimate estranging Enlightenment thing, to reduce God to an entity that, like the brain, can be weighed and compared pound to pound. But then once you have taken that plunge, it is hard to resist going the whole hog and asking literal questions: how much might he weigh, and whether his weight is constant and whether, like an Old Testament god such as Brecht's *Baal*, he might be prone to stuffing himself with food and drink, blowing out into a many-pounded god indeed? Is he middle class so that even if he is god of the fast food nation he can yet remain slim and trim, as is not only proper, nowadays, but is the sort of miracle that only he could pull off and that America sorely needs? Is he even a guy?

Of all organs, the brain strikes me as especially uncanny to look at and to hold and to eat, too. Is this because it is quote unquote the seat of con-

---

Originally presented at a small conference on science and religion at Duke University, January 2010; originally printed in Trigger93: The Word, vol. 1.

1. Emily Dickinson, *The Complete Poems of Emily Dickinson*, Pt. 1: *Life*, CXXVI (126) (Boston: Little, Brown, and Company, 1924).

sciousness, which must be very close to God, especially when you consider the very strange status of that piece of it called the pineal gland,
seen by different philosophers, such as René Descartes, as the guardian
of the threshold where matter and ideas, things and God meet? Ah! The
pineal gland, that good old friend lost in swirling deconstructing mists of
confusion, its importance way bigger than its diminutive size, more like
a syllable than a sound, like Kafka's doorman to the law who likes to keep
you waiting way past bedtime.

Well that was a long time ago, you say, so now I should, like a good scientist, bring you up to date and tell you about a professor who came to my
campus in Ann Arbor as a special guest of the Philosophy Department and
who was kind enough to give a little talk to the anthropologists on certain
aspects of the topic of his invention known as "sociobiology." When he was
done, a graduate student challenged his reduction of mind to matter, and
she did so in a rather persistent manner. The visitor brought out two words
that I recall well—talk about poetry! One was "preprint," which was new
to me, and the other was—well, you guessed it—our old friend the pineal
gland. He had a preprint with him, he said, gesturing vainly to his back
pocket, and went on to sketch in the miraculous role of the pineal gland—
what I call Kafka's guardian—in pulling off the greatest alchemical trick
of all time, converting chemical and electrical impulses into thoughts and
God knows what else God knows.

Poets must be shamans of a particular kind, conjuring and sleight of
hand being their tools of trade, and here I cannot but wonder at the relationship between "preprint" and pineal gland, as if the pineal gland is the
permanently preprinting device, that God-awesome potential behind all
potentiation, the dream and vision almost within grasp that, yes!, with a
little more of a nudge and a little more money from the National Science
Foundation, will—like infinitesimal calculus—keep on closing the gap between soul and electricity, thought and genes, mind and matter . . . such
that finally, on the Day of Judgment perhaps, we shall be able to fuse the
two into one, like cheese melting into the pizza crust.

I wonder, however, if reduction of this order can ever be achieved
without the miracle working pizza god? For as the professor reached for
his preprint, he became pale—perhaps the preprint was not there or was
only in the pre-preprint stage—and he slowly slid off his chair into a dead
faint. Boy, were his hosts in the Philosophy Department worried, running
around in circles looking helplessly for a wet handkerchief while casting

dirty looks at that graduate student who was basically doing nothing more than following graduate school protocol in going for the jugular, as they say. Others might call it murder, or at the least manslaughter, and still others sorcery. Slowly he recovered consciousness and was led away by his handlers to deliver, next day, a robust affirmation of faith in sociobiology. But you do have to wonder. Perhaps the pineal gland misfired or something? Who knows?

On the other hand, might this not have been a fortuitous ascent into the higher realms of consciousness whereby the soul escapes the body for a lofty purpose, thereby contributing in no small measure to the brilliance of his lecture the following day? Who knows. Poets must be shamans of a particular kind, conjuring and sleight of hand being their tools of trade, and of course picturing too, as in a blacked out lecture hall in an old Midwestern university where a slide show is going on sometime around 1980. Up on the stage a strongly built academic is in his three-piece suit lecturing on his favorite theme, ethnobotany, a field he claims to have invented or at least put on the map. The hall is large and full of people.

The slide show takes us to the Amazon looking for rubber for the US during World War II and then, lo and behold!, we come across some Indians with their strange hairdos and body paint and near nakedness. Why! They are taking drugs! Some rare snuff you get blown up you nose through a hollow bird bone the shape of a "Y."

In the dark, the lecturer is but a vague shadow manipulating the images that come out of nowhere to fall like blessed light on the screen. The face of one of those Indians now occupies the whole screen. It is a face covered with yellow-green mucus. He is cross-eyed and out of focus. Heaven forbid, he is taking a psychedelic drug. The hall is deathly quiet.

"They call this drug their god," says the man in the three-piece suit. His voice reverberates.

He pauses, a blur in the dark, "I will show you what their god is!"

Poets must be shamans of a particular kind, conjuring and sleight of hand being their tools of trade, along with their picturing. The screen goes black for a moment and is then filled with the most serene blue, that celestial blue of the ceilings of churches in the countryside in Colombia, that same celestial blue I saw repeatedly in medical school in Australia in biochemistry classes, the trick being that the white outline of the hexagonal benzene ring is thereby brilliantly set off and easy to read.

And here it was again. Twenty years had passed. And here it was again.

That same blue. That heavenly blue. And that same hexagon, albeit with a few more bells and whistles.

"This is their god!"

And there was their god. A hexagon ring on its bed of celestial blue. The audience gasped and tittered and I, who had also taken hallucinogens with the Indians in the Amazon, walked out, stumbling in the dark, leaving them to further enlightenment.

So by all means let us talk about science and religion, but first let us talk a little about the art of science including its shamanism and the art of out-shamanizing the other shaman, which is what most of shamanism is about anyway.

What the man in the three-piece suit did not get, at least consciously, and ditto the audience, was the stupendous fact that in replacing "their god" with a biochemical formula he was actually showing us his god and implicitly urging us to accept this god as ours.

The translation of god into a hexagon is pretty much the same as the preprint of the pineal gland in that in trying to close the gap by reducing god to a chemical, you become aware that the gap can never be closed. The cheese will not melt into the pizza. The magical thing—the formula—is itself just that: magical, a symbol, if you like, standing in for something else that leads to another something else ad nauseam. Hexagons all the way down.

Moreover the man in the three-piece suit is piggybacking on them naked Indians and their gods of the pre-print era. He uses them to cancel themselves out in place of science. But he does not realize that in canceling them out this way he is actually in need of their power—their symbolic power, if you like—so that as with Hegel's *aufhebung* he is utterly dependent on the ghost in the machine, the act he is reacting against, victim of the anxiety of influence that befalls us all. This is nothing more than the missionary position as well as that of the *conquistadores*, building churches on top of their temples.

Finally, I hardly need to bring to your attention the ritual upon which all this depends—the darkened room, the man with the magic wand (i.e., pointer, the magic of the slides, the abrupt montage action from the mucus smeared face to the celestial blue of chemistry, and of course the exotic nature of the subject matter, all mustered together to provide a mighty wallop).

Poets must be shamans of a particular kind, conjuring and sleight of hand being part of their trade, so it would only be fair for me to tell you about my own maladroit performance as an academic giving the lowdown on magic at the religion-science interface. It was many years ago in 1972 in the whitewashed colonial city of Popayán in southern Colombia and I was giving an academic talk—my very first—to an audience of students and professors in a room in the Casa Mosquera in the oldest university in the Americas. A job was being advertised in the Anthropology Department and I had elected as my title "Brujería y Estructura Social" (Witchcraft and Social Structure), having been impressed by two things that had happened to me recently. One was my discovery of sorcery and the other was my desperate search for enlightenment on this obscure and eerie topic—it never having been part of my orthodox Marxist sociological training at the LSE.

With the luxury of hindsight I now see that my lecture title was intended to impress my prospective audience with a finely balanced tension between mystery and science, as with the magical word "estructura" or "structure," the implication of that one word being that science had magic by the balls, so to speak.

When I got off the bus after a three-hour trip up the Andes from the hot sugarcane valley where I lived, I was taken aback to see plastered in bold black letters on yellow parchment on the venerable whitewashed walls all over town that a "Dr. Michael Taussig from the University of London" was going to give a talk on "Witchcraft and Social Structure." Later I realized that this advertising all over town was responsible for the large number of elderly women seated in the front rows of that room in the Casa Mosquera, silent as mice but with anticipation all over their faces. It turned out that they were witches themselves or attached to spirit centers of dubious repute.

Opening with a description of the poverty in the sugarcane areas, I used the word *barriga* to describe the swollen stomachs of a near majority of kids because of malnutrition and intestinal parasites. Like a shot, a professor of anthropology—who had extensive rice farms in that region and had written on tobacco among Colombian Indians for the same ethnobotany department that the man in the three-piece suit had founded—stood up shouting that he didn't want to hear any more of this demagoguery and that the word *barriga* was of vulgar usage. I was staggered. But no sooner had he spat out what he had to say than a bunch of vociferous students stood up and shouted at him that he was the demagogue! I have no idea how I finished my talk but I do recall the eyes of the elderly ladies in the front row glistening.

However, I did finish, to tepid applause, only to be met by a strident call to arms from the back of the room. With the voice of a preacher, a man in his thirties implored the audience to take account of the work of Sir Isaac Newton. "Once you reckon with that," he thundered, "you will realize there is no such thing as witchcraft." The women in front were as spellbound as I was. "This must be like what happened in the days of the Enlightenment," I thought to myself, "in Paris, London, and Königsberg." And I recalled Newton's abiding interest in magic and the likes of John Dee, necromancer and astrologer to the queen.

To say the least, I was confused and a little scared by the passions aroused as one of the elderly women approached me, smiling, with her card advertising a spirit center. With my title advertised all around town— "Witchcraft and Social Structure"—I had come looking for a job as a scientific anthropologist. To polish my wares I had industriously applied the poetics-of-mystery versus the revelatory powers-of-science, allowing the concept of "structure" to do the heavy lifting, so as to allow science the final say. And what had happened? The witches took me as one of their own and the students, who had at first rushed to my defense, finished up by throwing Marxist and Enlightenment stones, identifying me in the same way as did the elderly ladies, as a spokesman for witchcraft. Everything was twisted upside down. Truly witchcraft is a trying phenomenon. There seemed no room for the neutral, dispassionate observer because description was conflated with advocacy—first by the large rice farm owner, professor of anthropology, interpreting my description as demagogic leftism, and later by the students, or some of them, conflating my description with advocacy of something that, according to them, did not exist or, if it did, should not. Their dilemma was that of outlawing something that in their eyes did not exist. This must have been the same dilemma facing administration in the colonies of the European powers. What good would Sir Isaac Newton provide me in such a situation, especially as I was now on the side of the witches?

Poets must be shamans of a particular kind, conjuring and sleight of hand being part of their trade, and here I was, the scientist, caught by poetics and hung out to dry. Let us review the evidence.

First, the sociobiologist, the ethnobotanist, and I myself, were all operating in fields overlapping with, or fully within, the human and social sciences. Second, we were each of us operating in one of the preeminent theaters of scientific discussion, namely the lecture theater. Third, each one of us acted like shamans in using our trick of the trade—language, our mumbo jumbo such as the pineal gland, the "preprint," the biochemical formula, and in my case the ever-ready workhorse of "structure." Fourth, in each case we were addressing issues of consciousness; and in my case and that of the ethnobotanist, that of religion and magic, making a real mess of things. We were novices because we had gotten the science-magic thing ballsed up. We were totally taken in by scientism and the mythology of the detached observer, oblivious to our social and mythic contexts and the impact our selves made in those contexts.

The most stupendous aspect was that we were implicitly using magic to contain magic. We were using ritual and theater to contain ritual and theater. And we were using poetry to out-maneuver the poetry inherent to all human understanding and activity. And we failed. We were not up to the task. Maybe the ethnobotanist got away with it. You can't beat a magic lantern show and he had enormous prestige and the right audience, young science jocks like himself. And plants are guarantees of innocence and honesty, not to mention beauty.

But we were not good enough because we were confused without knowing we were confused. We thought we were fighting the good fight against obscurantism and mumbo jumbo, magic, and religion, etc., in the name of genetics, Darwin, biochemistry, and structure. But willy-nilly without being aware, we were actually practicing the same stealth arts we thought we were fighting, and from which we thought we were immune. If only we had started afresh, with the poets, and listened to Emily Dickinson, "The brain is wider than the sky,"

For, put them side by side,
The one the other will include
With ease, and you beside.[2]

---

2. Dickinson, *Complete Poems*, pt. 1.

# Don Miguel

My name is Michael but when I got to Colombia people called me Miguel. I arrived in November 1969 to join the revolution. I was twenty-nine years old with a medical degree and a modest scholarship from the University of London to research the insane horror of the *Violencia*, a Rwanda-like bloodletting that occurred in the mid-twentieth century. I was to write a book based on what I found.

My first taste of Colombia was the pounding rain in Panama followed by the glare of Barranquilla on the Caribbean coast. I found a cheap hotel, grateful for a place to deposit my enormous suitcase filled with books by the likes of Karl Marx with their covers ripped off so as to make it harder, so I hoped, to identify them in case of police inspection. I was prepared. In London I had even gotten myself a pair of steel-rimmed spectacles, free, from the marvelous British Health Service, so that I could be all the more carefree when scouting with the guerrilla, whom I knew nothing about but with whom I felt bound to connect pretty soon and so be part of the onward march envisioned by Mao , the long march of the countryside encircling the city, analogous with the Third World encircling the First.

When I saw the tabloids neatly spread page by lewd page on the city pavement by the vendors, I started to wonder. Photographs of mutilated corpses in all manner of poses shared the pavement alongside photographs of naked women. Pedestrians would stop and look with curiosity even though, God knows, every day the same sort of images were laid out. It was like the peep shows on 42nd Street, New York, only you didn't have to pay anything and on this street in Barranquilla—the violence had as much or more space than the sex.

It was reassuring to meet up with a chemical engineer working in nearby Cartagena, a Colombian by birth and education who, so it was said in London by college mates, had revolutionary contacts. I remember him now more than forty years later, a sweet yet serious guy with a precise manner, handsome with reddish hair and glasses. I clutched at him as my salvation in an environment that had suddenly become turbulent. He offered me no contacts. But he gave me some sense of familiarity and the feeling, vague as it was, that my mission was not altogether a fantasy. But, of course, it was a fantasy, and quite a dangerous one at that.

When I reached gloomy Bogotá in the cold highlands deep inland, I heard how university students who had rushed off to join the ELN guerrilla had been executed by the guerrilla for daring to have ideas of their own and not submit to revolutionary discipline. The wildly popular priest, Camillo Torres, a professor of the newly fangled subject of sociology at the national university, an intellectual and not a soldier by training or character, had recently gone to the forest to join with the ELN and had been ignominiously killed by a sergeant in the Colombian army after a few minutes in his first effort at combat. The army hid his body, just as happened to Che Guevara in Bolivia farther south.

Four months later I was well into what now looks like "fieldwork" in a small hot town in western Colombia. A letter of introduction to one of the town's doctors, active in recent years in a movement challenging the local power elite known somewhat affectionately, as in every town in Colombia, as *La Rosca*, or the Doughnut, assured me a warm welcome, at least from some people. One of them offered a space to rent at the back of a single-story brick house. My companion, Anna Rubbo, who had forsaken an interesting job as an architect in London with the famous Swedish company of Ave Arup, came and joined me and had two walls broken down to create a wonderful loft-like space. We shared the patio with a truck. There was no drinkable water and the toilet was a hole in the ground.

Never having actually read much anthropology— after all, my fields were sociology and revolution—I had no clear idea what fieldwork meant. Later I learned that this was quite common even for anthropologists. Fieldwork might be their *rite de passage*, alone in a foreign land like Jesus in the Wilderness, but it was nevertheless an experience which, so it seems, it is important to enter into blind without advice from those who went before. It is the same as learning to swim by being thrown in at the deep end.

So there we were swimming, quite well, actually, and having loads of fun. As strangers and objects of curiosity we brought out the best among our hosts. It was important, I believe, that we had nothing very concrete to offer, so long as we had a plausible story about why we were there which, in my case, was to write a book about the history of the town from the abolition of slavery to the present day. True to our then rather simplistic sense of class oppression, we tended to shun the local commercial class running the town and got involved instead with the single mothers gleaning in the fields of the rich farmers, the immigrant canecutters and loaders from the far-off Pacific Coast, and the local peasants.

The "deep end" idea worked. Anna was fascinated by the flexibility of the extended family house of adobe and bamboo. She learned the construction techniques and pondered the startling lessons this organic peasant architecture held for professional architecture and state housing plans which rarely took into account local knowledge and ways of life. We sought out stories about *La Violencia* and about the new sugar plantations that appeared at the same time as the *violencia*, in the 1950s, spreading like wildfire over the tiny farms of the descendants of African slaves. With the abolition of slavery in 1851, the latter had squatted on their former owners' lands and made extraordinary tree farms, ecological seven day wonders, replicating the tropical forest. These farms were composed of trees of cacao, plantains, oranges, mandarins, zapotes, cachimbo, and bread fruit. In the early twentieth century, coffee was added to the mix. It was these farms that the new, open field large scale agriculture of the wealthy white class in the cities, was bent on demolishing so as to plant sugar. Looking back now with eyes opened to negative consequences of western-style open field agriculture, it is easy to see how far ahead of their time these peasants farms were. But back then when we came to the area, they were seen as obstacles to progress.

I got absorbed in collecting genealogies on large sheets of paper, which turned out to be a marvelous way of learning history as stories(what's the difference?) and studying those wonderful peasant farms, keeping close track of the harvesting that took place every two weeks, the amount of labor required (very little), and weighing the leaves that mounted on the forest floor impeding weed growth, providing abundant fertilizer, and smoothing out fluctuations in rainfall.

After four months of whirlwind activity we needed a break and went to Bogotá to write uninterruptedly. There we met, among others, an English architect, Alec Bright, the director of the famous Gold Museum located on the second story of the Banco de la República. A charming person, with an angular face, fair hair, and a gentle smile, he took a deep interest in what we were doing and offered plenty of advice which was all the more convincing because it was clear he empathized with the people among whom we were now living. He could picture. He could imagine the situation. For he too had, as they say, "been there." Only later did I appreciate how special Anna and I were, too, like anthropological informants, fresh from the field with loads of raw stories and inexperience calling out for old hands to channel in the right direction.

All the more reason that we took to heart his amazement when, in answer to his question, we answered that No! we had met with neither the Bishop nor the Governor of Cauca, the province in which "our" little town was set.

"Oh! You must do that!," he insisted, "That's the way things are done in Colombia."

We felt otherwise. Things were going so well for us without having to shake hands or mix with important people for whom we often felt a visceral dislike by virtue of the fact that they were "important." But Alec was a force to be reckoned with. His was the voice of experience. We were mere novices. Like us he was from outside the society, from England, a comforting zone of origin when far away from it, and married to a Colombian. He, therefore, had the double advantage of seeing the society with the insights guaranteed the foreigner, grafted on to the insights bequeathed someone born into it.

So we vowed to rectify our mistake and pay a visit to the Bishop and the Governor. After all, it could be interesting to visit these people. Social analysis surely required seeing things from the top as well as from the bottom of society? Before my arrival in Colombia, I had imbibed in England the lessons of the exciting new Marxist historiography, as in the books by E. P. Thompson and Eric Hobsbawm, seeing history as largely created by the exploitation and resistance of working people whose lives were conveniently forgotten as time went by. Thus it became an important task of the new breed of historians to rectify matters and set the record straight by focusing more on "ordinary" people and their workday lives.

But in Berkeley, California, in 1969 on my way to Colombia, I had received a painful surprise. My enthusiasm was doused by some graduate students in the Department of History, specializing on Latin America, who suggested to me that the more appropriate task for intellectuals who wished for a more fair society was to focus not on the poor and oppressed but on the powerful. The Berkeley anthropologist Laura Nader, sister of Ralph Nader, had even given this a name. "Studying up," she called it, not "down." I had to admit they had a point, now more than ever. What struck me as strange was how two equally radical schools could have such diametrically opposed strategies. What appears as a radical objective to scholars, including historians, would seem to depend on subtle nuances in their own particular histories. Marxism in Britain, for instance, had a very different feel to it than in the US where, to the trauma of McCarthyism (now being repeated by the Bush administration's "patriot act"), was added the energy of the 1960s struggle for racial equality, the antiwar movement, and the flowering of anarchist sentiment in Haight-Ashbury.

As for studying up, it wasn't as if we didn't have any well-to-do friends, in Bogotá, for instance, or the charming, gentle, chain-smoking Don Victor Torres from Cali, with a snappy straw hat who drove through our town in his new Toyota Jeep, the first in the area to displace the smaller Willys, and who worked as chief administrator for some wealthy sugarcane interests, but not the ones with mills in our area. We liked each other straight off. He had run into us in a lonely part of the countryside and suggested where we could buy a horse from a friend, which is how we acquired the magnificent, deep-chested Paso Fino, on whom we bestowed the name of Ben Hall, a famous nineteenth-century Australian bandit, or bushranger. It was through Victor that we met important players in the new rural economy, such as the manager of *el ingenio Argentina*, between Ortigal and Corinto, a sugar mill that, according to prices on the market, could switch from sugar to producing panela, three-inch square blocks of brown, unrefined sugar, same as *gur* in India, and pretty much the basis of the diet of poor people in Colombia. It was fascinating to hear their stories, like secrets, as far as we were concerned, about the noose agribusiness was drawing ever tighter around the necks of the poor.

When they talked about black people they would purse their lips in what they thought was an imitation and describe them as terribly lazy and dirty. But at least the blacks were "open," unlike the Indians who, although supposed to work hard, were sneaky and tight-lipped. . . . They hung out when the cool breeze came without fail late afternoons in Cali at their informal *club de vagos*, "club of the bums," located in their friend's gun shop, and they once took us to a party at the country club with its drab swimming pool and spreading lawns. Booze and gallantry was flowing in abundance.

The men knew everything, while their girlfriends of the moment provided the decoration, flaunting tight butts, yards of silky hair, and high birdlike twittering voices. The afternoon dragged on in clouds of cigarettes and liquor, mutual adoration and bad jokes. All seemed mighty rich or sons and daughters of the rich, or, in some cases, skillful hangers-on with some submissive trick to play so as to earn their keep.

So, even though our overriding inclination was to avoid such people, we took Alec's injunction to heart and next time I was in the provincial capital, the old slave-owning city of Popayán in which every stately home and impoverished dwelling, by decree or custom, is painted white, I called on the governor, a block away from the archive where we had discovered a cache of nineteenth-century letters written by slave owners to their *mayordomos* concerning the running of their estates where "our" town was located.

The governor's name indicated he was probably of noble birth, there being three ruling-class family names in Popayán: the Valencias, the Mosqueras, and the Arboledas. These were the largest slave-owning families of the colony of Nueva Granada which was even bigger than present-day Colombia.. One of the living Valencias, name of Pio, at that time rector of the Univerdad de Cali, was said to be a member of the Colombian Communist Party and to have sold a goodly part of his land for cheap housing for the poor. By contrast, his brother, Guillermo, stalwart of the Conservative Party, had become President of the Republic in the early 1960s at which time the US launched aerial bombardments, some say with napalm, against the so-called red republics in the center of the country. Located in the southern reaches of the Magdalena Valley, hugging the slopes of the *Cordilleras*, these "republics" began as self-defense settlements formed during *La Violencia* by peasants of the Liberal Party fleeing from the Conservative Party which had control of the armed forces, the police, and loads of paramilitaries as well. In this situation the self-defense settlements gravitated leftward away from the primordial sentiments of the old political party set-up, toward communism, a doctrine which in some important respects they had already put into practice anyway so as to survive in a collective manner but somewhat an embarrassment to the Colombian Communist Party—Moscow oriented to a fault—which had no place in its theory for peasant revolution.

All of some thirty-five years of age, seated behind a large desk in an empty, high-ceilinged, room, the baby-faced governor demanded of me my business. I told him I was a sociologist wishing to study the history of the slaves after abolition in the south of the Cauca Valley, and how the freed slaves adapted to the commercialization of agriculture in the twentieth century. Upon demonstrating my letter of introduction from the University of London, appropriately studded with colored ribbons and red wax seals, he looked down his nose and informed me with withering contempt that he knew all about socialism.

That was pretty much the end of our meeting. I went back to the archive and buried myself in family letters and documents issued by notaries, mostly on yellow linen-based paper and written in ink that never seemed to fade, not like the later nineteenth-century paper which crumbled at the touch.

Every now and again a man in a gray cotton coat would meticulously sweep the floor around the table, his head inclined to one side. Later I was told he belonged to the communist party and he had the job of spying on researchers, especially the foreign ones, of whom, in those years, there were few. No doubt he was spreading the story that Anna and I worked for the CIA. But then the director of the archive, a small, neatly dressed man in his fifties with impeccable manners, a proud descendant of the Arboledas, was spreading a different story. He was telling his pals in the exclusive Club Popayán that we were part of a cabal searching for disused gold mines.

I felt someone tapping my shoulder. A creepy-looking guy in a suit and the body of a leech said softly, "Can you come with me, please?" He was from the DAS, what is often referred to as "the secret police." The thought flashed through my mind: the governor! Sociology means socialism! The governor was right, pretty much, but that was accidental. Or was it? The shade of uncle Guillermo Valencia with his aerial bombardment of socialists loomed large. And hadn't the rebel priest Camilo Torres been among the founding professors of sociology at Colombia's Universidad Nacional but a handful of years back? Hadn't he ended up a *guerrillero*, his name a graffiti wherever there was a suitable wall, imploring people to rise up and fight?

With images of thumbscrews and wet towels hovering before me I meekly followed this wretched emissary to his headquarters where I was politely questioned, asked for my passport and letters of introduction, and asked to explain why I was in Colombia, where I lived, and so forth. Yet polite or not, I was plenty scared and next day we decided to return to "our" town, three hours by bus north into the hot country where we could be with people we knew and plan our next move.

Getting off the bus by the Rio Palo, we walked over the bridge where scores of women and young girls were washing clothes by the grassy bank, then crossed the plaza by the church where I entered the bakery owned by Don Miguel who had come from Lebanon many years before. Nowdays, thanks to the sugar mills and paper mill upstream, the river is a dimunitive relic of what it once was and the pollution so fearsome that nobody would wash clothes in it.

As I waited for Don Miguel to wrap my bread he said, "Funny thing happened yesterday. Two guys came in and asked me if I was Don Miguel! I said 'Sure! That's me. *A la orden.*' Then they asked to see my passport! Can you imagine? I haven't had a passport in twenty years!" He shook his head in disbelief.

"So what?" I thought vaguely to myself. It seemed like his story had some hidden meaning but that was of no real concern to me. He was a personage. A small-town fixture. The owner of the panadería, Don Miguel.

We hurried down the dusty street to our lodging. There was little traffic in those days, mainly old trucks carrying material for the sugar plantations or horse-drawn carts laden with gravel from the river or with food from the market held twice a week on Wednesdays and Sundays. I went by the corner where the *prendería* or pawn shop, owned by a whiteman from Antioquia was, as usual, doing a roaring business. On the opposite corner were clusters of women and kids waiting for a truck to carry them out of town to the cocoa and coffee groves around Guyabal and Guachene where flourishing peasant farms were being laid flat for sugarcane. They were carrying wicker baskets with their weekly provisions such as rice and sugar, a minute lump of fatty meat with bone wrapped in a green leaf, a tiny packet of cumin, salt, onions, some lard, and maybe a handful of homemade spindly candles. The women draped their heads to cut down the heat of the sun. Others walked straight-backed like fashion models carrying enormous weights on top of their heads.

When we reached home, Marlene Vargas, our landlady, greeted us without her expansive smile. "A funny thing happened yesterday," she said. "Two guys came and asked if Don Miguel lived here. I said yes, he did, and then they asked if they could go into your room! I lied, saying you had taken the key, and they said they would come back."

I cursed Alec Bright. Why had we listened to him about the need to work from the top down? Why hadn't we trusted our gut instincts? Of course it wasn't his fault. But now something had to be done. To resolve the situation we had to go back to the top. What irony!

Flying to Bogotá over snow-capped volcanoes with the plane at times dropping straight down in the turbulence was a relief. Our first port of call was Mario Laserna who had been recommended to me by a historian at Oxford, Malcolm Deas, who had with great generosity given me names of people to look up in Colombia. Mario had at one time been a Conservative Party aspirant for the Presidency of Colombia, had co-founded what became the country's elite Universidad de los Andes, and had written an important book on the peculiar nature of the Colombian state as the conjunction of the two political parties, Liberal and Conservative, which in effect ran the country in lieu of a state. His family had large rice farms in the Magdalena valley near Ibague and earlier he had made it possible for me to visit there.

His office in downtown Bogotá was in a narrow and sleazy street, hardly a fashionable area. The interiors were wan with narrow corridors and dark paneling. When Anna and I entered his office on the third or fourth floor there was a peasant from Tumaco, slum port on the mangrove flats of the Pacific Coast, lifting up an empty hemp bag called a *costal* that the peasants use to carry produce such as corn on the back of ponies and mules. Spread out in all directions on the dirty nondescript carpet, the color of moth's wings, were fabulous pre-Colombian ceramics—half-human, half-animal—with some profiles of African-looking heads, as well. Some were chipped or broken.

Having made his purchase, Mario was able to turn to us and, on hearing our story, hesitated, then telephoned a friend of his, a colonel, none other than the head of the DAS, or "secret police." My heart leapt. This was power! In those days the phones were even worse than today. But he eventually got through. "Grab a taxi, " he said, "and go to this address."

The taxi seemed to take forever threading its way south through the horrendous traffic along Carrera Décima till, as memory serves me, we reached a seven- or eight-story stone building. We walked in circles through this dark labyrinth of arches and stone corridors unable to find our way. There were many men walking in all directions. They wore dark rumpled suits and had greasy hair. They had shifty eyes, a morose air, and hunched their heads into their shoulders, somewhat like the Tumaco human-animal ceramic hybrids we had seen on Mario's carpet but half an hour before.

The colonel, a thin elegant man with a tired air occupied a huge office with a large L-shaped desk. The blinds were drawn. It was dark. A two-way radio sat to one side and the colonel was receiving a crackling message, hard to hear on account of the static. It seemed to be an agent reporting to him from one of Colombia's most remote provinces on the Venezuelan border about a missing operative. "We haven't . . . seen him in two weeks . . . we talked with the wife . . ." And the message died. So much for the efficiency of the secret police.

We sat down in front of the desk. The colonel heard us through with his eyes narrowing. He leaned back and carefully enunciated: "*Pueblo pequeño, infierno grande,*" which means "Small towns make for huge hells," although it sounds better in Spanish.

Well, that seemed good, like he was being a sociologist not blaming any particular person but rather the social system itself. It also sounded as if we were dealing with a man of the world who had a decent sense of humor, not your usual macho torturer running what was undoubtedly a nasty organization. It was calming to find it had a human face.

"But," he continued, "people like you give us a lot of trouble." I went cold. "Only the other day a French anthropologist living in the Magdalena Medio left to join the guerrilla!," and he raised his eyebrows as if asking a question. Anna and I were shocked at this dereliction of anthropological duty (long before the Colombian sociologist Orlando Fals-Borda came up with the proposal of an activist sociolology after visiting us in Cauca). The colonel sighed and berated us with a lenghty list of problems young foreigners in the back blocks presented his security apparatus, then ushered us abruptly out of his office leaving us to descend those Escher-like staircases filled with rushing, dark-suited, hybrid men, half-animal, half human.

Years later I walked past this DAS building. It had been converted into luxury condos as Colombia became wealthy thanks to cocaine. In my melodramatic way I imagined what it must be like going to sleep in a condo with the screams of torture victims coming out of the walls.

Thus history passes unnoticed.

Malcolm had also given me the name of the young political attaché at the British Embassy, Keith Morris, whom I liked enormously. He was smart with a lively interest in the ways of the world, had a Spanish wife, and was always dashing off to different parts of Colombia to listen to politicians on the stump and no doubt report to his superiors where the country was headed. That was something that always impressed me with this class of mind, how it could generalize and summarize in pithy, strategic, sentences whereas I get caught in images and details. Keith had a deeply rooted attachment to the country. This became apparent decades later when out of the blue I came across a passionate article in one of the British dailies by Sir Keith Morris, now retired, if I remember correctly, making the case for legalizing drugs as a way of stopping the terrible violence the drug trade had unleashed throughout Colombia. It tore his heart. He seemed like David hurling his puny missiles against the US Goliath and all clean living citizens like Nancy Reagan with her "Just Say No" logo that I saw in a photograph on William Burroughs's fridge door. I remember it was Keith who drew a parallel with Homer when I told him sometime in 1970, or 1971, about a blind, eighty-year-old peasant poet in our town, Don Tomás Zapata, who had composed a lengthy poem on the local manifestations of *La Violencia.*

In that first year, before I cast my lot more firmly with left wing activistsm in Colombia, I felt comfortable with the embassy crowd, or at least that part of it. We used to sometimes lunch together weekdays in Bogotá, delightful occasions, full of good humor, which could not end until the immensely kind Colombian, Julio T., a pear-shaped man with a small moustache, was asked if he wanted *tinto* (meaning a small black coffee) so that he could reply:"No, thanks, it will stop me sleeping when I get back to work!"

What exactly Julio was meant to do in his office was a mystery to me. I seem to remember something like Public Relations, but that can mean anything. He had earlier worked in the US embassy and spoke a little English. Married to a middle-aged woman from the US, he gave the impression of someone who had seen better times, economically. He was, however, blessed with many friends in high places and I came to believe he was, because of that, a remarkably effective trouble-shooter for the Brits in the embassy for whom it might appear socially, not to mention, politically, awkward to make certain telephone calls and work the media (as we call it, today).

It was he, perhaps in consultation with Keith, who came up with the idea of getting in touch with the head of public relations of the *Banco Cafetero* to help solve our problem with the secret police and the Governor of Cauca. At that time coffee—not cocaine, heroin, or petroleum—was the leading export and Colombia essentially meant coffee, if not vice versa. Hence the *Banco Cafetero* packed a punch. The man in question, so it turned out, was none other than another Valencia from Popayán, another son of the former President who had allowed the US to try to bomb away the red republics. What's more, he was married to a British woman and there existed cordial ties with the embassy. His name, as I remember was Felipe, or Pedro, but I could be wrong.

Anna and I went to visit him on a high floor of the bank in downtown Bogotá on the Jiménez. It was a sunny day and the blue skies were a good omen. Anna, I should add, is very beautiful and elegant and this as much as her sincerity and honesty was probably as effective as anything our powerful friends were able to do.

Felipe listened courteously, thought for a moment, and said he would write a letter to someone in "our" town—and this I couldn't believe—to José Arévalo!

This was a man we had never met. Perhaps one of us had seen him skulking along the street in "our" town but we had not known who it was, although we had heard his name once or twice. People seemed afraid of him. He lived isolated on the other side of the Palo River, the side where nobody but he and the mayordomo of some absentee landlords ( the Holguines) lived. His house spoke of another culture. It was raised a little off the ground and had rusty mosquito screens all around, something we had never seen on other houses and that I myself found profoundly depressing. He had been the military mayor of the town during *La Violencia* in the early 1950s and it was put about he had killed a lot of people. He belonged, naturally, to the Conservative Party. The vast majority of the town and surrounding areas belonged to the Liberal Party. They were black. He was white.

The letter was ready the next day. It began something like, "*Muy Estimado Señor*, I will never forget the mangoes you sent my father in Popayán" and proceeded with the hope that he, José Arévalo, would be able to look after us.

Back in Julio's office in the embassy a photographer with a big flash bulb was ready for us. Julio put Anna and I either side of the Colombian Boy Scout shield he had hanging head height on the wall. It turned out he was the head of the Boy Scouts! The three of us assembled. The flash popped. Then Julio jumped aside and the photographer popped again with just me and Anna and the Boy Scout shield centering the picture. Julio surprised me. He was nimble for a man of his girth. Yet I don't think that is why I remember his acrobatics so vividly. It was what I felt, rightly or wrongly, to be his duplicity that shocked me. Having brilliantly set up his theater, he had to spirit himself out of it as well. He was the puppet master. We were his puppets or, rather, the Colombian public was his puppet.

Next day the newspapers carried the photograph, the one without Julio, black and white, our heads half-turned, facing each other across the Boy Scout shield. It bore a long caption saying how we were in Colombia to carry out a scientific study for the benefit of the nation. We both looked very handsome. It was a great photograph. It was time to go home.

In our town a few days later I was stopped outside the *alcaldía* or town hall by someone congratulating me on the photograph. The street *there* is filled with all manner of petitioners and semi-employed lawyer types awaiting clients to guide through the bureaucracy. News spreads like fire there.

As the day cooled off toward evening we walked over the river to deliver the fateful letter from Felipe to José Arévalo. He received us cordially, an austere old man still physically powerful and astute. He told us Felipe had actually called him by telephone to talk about us. He served coffee and we chatted about nothing much for about an hour and he invited us back for lunch the following day. Later I heard from someone in town that Felipe had also called the *personero*, a high-ranking official in local administration.

We arrived for lunch a little late to find him and his eldest daughter by a second marriage both anxious that we might not come. We sat in the same chairs in the same configuration as the day before. The three of us went into another room to eat, attended by the daughter; chicken soup, chicken, rice, and Coca-Cola. We talked for two and half hours, some of the time interesting, with him dominating the conversation but not its direction. He knew loads of local history and, regarding *La Violencia*, he was the *alcalde maravilloso*—the kick-ass mayor—for six whole years! It was he who kept things under control. "When you get one man in the chain of bandits," he told us, "then you can break it by following the chain along." "Oh yes! It was dangerous here. Five inspectors were killed in one day!"

I had forgotten this conversation until today when by extraordinary luck I found two and half pages of single-spaced notes typed up in duplicate on my baby Olivetti dated November 7, 1970 (Sat.). My memory was quite different. My memory was that we had sat in stony silence with a tight-lipped José Arévalo in stuffy heat behind rusty mosquito screens, that it was agonizingly awkward, and that we were, both parties, playing an elaborate party game no less than the one Julio had played in the British Embassy where we were photographed. Having lunch with José Arévalo was no less a charade. We all performed our roles beautifully as if the entire event was somehow self-generated and not the outcome of forces set into motion by powerful figures and unholy phantoms—such as the sons of presidents, foreign embassies, and secret police. Some ten years later after that lunch I heard that José Arévalo had mysteriously disappeared.

I also read in those miraculously discovered two and half pages that our benefactor's name was neither Felipe nor Pedro, but Pedro Felipe, which brings me back to my own name, Don Miguel, and how strange I find it that the secret police, as I describe them, would call on the Lebanese baker in the town plaza simply because his name was Don Miguel and ask him for his passport as if he was me! "*Pueblo pequeño, infierno grande*," indeed! How could they be so dumb? How had they gotten to the bakery anyway? Did they walk around the plaza asking for Don Miguel? Sounds idiotic, but that must have been what happened. And why didn't I myself put it all together right there and then?

They were relatively peaceful and innocent times for Colombia. It wasn't till ten years later when the M-19 guerrilla stole the army's weapons on New Year's Eve 1980 in the mountain behind Bogotá, and left a note, "Happy New Year and Happy New Arms"—*Feliz año nuevo y armas nuevas*—and the FARC guerrilla came out of its long period of rest, that the government crackdown began, the torturers were let loose, and dissidents jailed under hideous conditions. As for the drug scene, in those days, cocaine was non-existent and the marijuana wonderfully romantic, associated with fruit eating, non-bathing, hippies in colorful gear lying spread-eagled across the bed stuporose for days if not months in cheap hotels in Popayán by the marketplace after being driven out of small mountain towns by mayors making a name for themselves purging the Devil.

Given the relative peace, the idea of some bumbling secret police wandering lost around the plaza of a small hot country town pathetically asking for Don Miguel does not appear unbelievable, but nevertheless it does make you realize how most of us grant police the world over with far more efficiency than they have.

It also makes me wonder about the connections between names and memory. I have been surprised, indeed astounded, as to the way, once I started setting this story down in writing, forty-four years after the event, I had what seemed like total recall for names, and vivid pictures swam into my mind of people and places. Perhaps I should rephrase this. I am surprised at the feeling of confidence I had that I was accurately recalling lost time. It was as if I had tugged at some rip-cord of memory and, like a silken parachute descending through the clouds of the past, I had in my flight caught the blue skies of memory. They filled out the delicate fabric that kept me sailing through the air.

Unlike Marcel Proust I bit no *madeleine*. Of course Proust found magic in names, such as the color that emerged with the name Guermantes, a name whose aura penetrated much of French history, he tells us, and the very sense of value. Proust's recovery of time is magical because it concerns things to which consciousness paid little heed. In my case here, however, it seems the opposite; that the things recalled were subject to a piercing consciousness at the time they were experienced.

What comes to me by way of the *memoire involontaire* is due to a name, or rather a translation of my name into a foreign language and hence a translation of my sense of myself. With that can also come a change of a person's sense of being.

It is this transfer point that was engaged so forcefully for me by my almost chance encounter with Don Miguel, the Lebanese baker, himself translated from the Middle East to Colombia for the rest of his life. A whole complicated setup of social classes and races is now lodged in my being, as Proust would have it, thanks to this tiny instant of confusion in names and identities. Is this my madeleine?

In fieldwork, about which I now count myself as one of the initiated, so to speak, being one of those people who made it through, you learn after a long, long time, that the famous "method" of *participant-observation* tends to be weighted toward the observation end of things and, what's more, tends not, according to the profession, to allow much by way of self-observation. What you learn is that because of class and race barriers, what I would call "true" participation is rare and unforgettable, but that the "stranger-effect," being a foreigner, makes this a lot easier. Some anthropologists, perhaps the great majority, make these barriers into a virtue, claiming that such participation is irrelevant and romantic, that we should study not ourselves, not psychology, not the anthropologist-native interaction, but something as vast and nebulous as "culture" (see Clifford Geertz's introduction to Malinowski's diaries, for example). But I really only learned about peasant agriculture, for instance, when, together with my peasant friend Robier Uzuriaga, we rented a small plot and cultivated it. This I call "participation;" participation in the sweat and hopes of labor, participation in the being of the plants and the soil, the rain and the bugs, and participation in hard-headed economics of prices of inputs and harvests, as well as having to forge a practical relationship with the adjoining peasants who became to me very different and multifaceted people once I stopped asking them questions as an anthropologist and became a cultivator. As they say, it got "real," and the same applies to our getting involved with peasant farmers in an organization called ANUC planning the invasion of a large estate just north of Villarica in 1971 so as to take over the land. (How times have changed! At least in the Cauca Valley.)

Similarly, in the case of the governor and the secret police, Anna and I were far more participants than detached observers. We were fully engaged in an anxious, at times frightening, zigzagging chase through the society so as to assuage the paranoia of the state we had inadvertently stung into action. *We had become objects in our own story*. That is why I feel I remember so much. That is why it has been not only easy but strangely pleasurable to tell this story. And that is also why this is analogous to biting the madeleine which, after all, is but another form of participant-observation. As I said at the beginning, my name is Michael but when I got to Colombia people called me Miguel.

# INDEX